The Duality of Laughter and Tears

Ultra Modern Life Philosophy, Volume 1

SANDEEP CHAVAN

Published by SANDEEP CHAVAN, 2024.

While every precaution has been taken in the preparation of this book, the publisher assumes no responsibility for errors or omissions, or for damages resulting from the use of the information contained herein.

THE DUALITY OF LAUGHTER AND TEARS

First edition. December 2, 2024.

Copyright © 2024 SANDEEP CHAVAN.

ISBN: 979-8230873112

Written by SANDEEP CHAVAN.

Table of Contents

1: The Enigma Begins 1
2: Faces in the Crowd 7
3: The Lull 17
4: Chasing Shadows 25
5: The Dreamer's Dilemma 30
6: The Turning Point 41
7: Into the Unknown 46
8: The Gathering 55
9: Stories Around the Fire 60
10: A Mirror to the Soul 65
11: The Silent Retreat 77
12: The Solitary Path 85
13: Embracing the Puzzle 91
14: The Return Home 102
A Message to My Readers 108

To the dreamers and achievers,The ones who chase success yet yearn for something deeper.To the restless hearts of Silicon Valley and beyond,May you find the courage to pause, reflect, and seek the joy that lies in the balance of ambition and contentment.

This book is for you—the successful but seeking,May it guide you toward laughter, embrace your tears,And help you discover the profound happiness hidden in life's imperfect moments.

With hope and gratitude,Sandeep Chavan

"In the pursuit of ambition, do not lose sight of the quiet truths that make us human. In the duality of laughter and tears, we find the essence of life's meaning."

– Sandeep Chavan

Disclaimer

This book is a work of fiction. While it draws inspiration from universal human experiences and philosophical concepts, the characters, events, and settings are products of the author's imagination. Any resemblance to actual persons, living or deceased, or real events, locations, or organizations is purely coincidental.

The ideas and reflections presented in this book are intended to provoke thought and introspection. They should not be considered professional advice, guidance, or solutions for personal, psychological, or philosophical matters. Readers are encouraged to consult appropriate professionals for specific concerns or challenges in their lives.

The author has made every effort to present information accurately and responsibly. However, any interpretations or conclusions drawn by readers are their own, and the author assumes no liability for how this content is understood or applied.

This book's intent is to inspire dialogue, self-reflection, and exploration of the complexities of human existence. It is not intended to dictate any particular worldview or philosophy but rather to offer perspectives for consideration.

Thank you for embracing this journey with an open mind and heart.

Preface

The Duality of Laughter and Tears: Finding Silence in the Chaos of Silicon Valley

In a world driven by endless notifications, relentless ambition, and the race to innovate, we often find ourselves teetering on the edge of fulfillment and emptiness. For years, I believed that success was defined by the metrics we proudly showcase—career milestones, accolades, financial stability. Living and thriving in Silicon Valley, the epicenter of technological advancement and the dreamland of ambitious minds, I thought I had it all figured out. Yet, beneath the surface of achievement lay a quiet yearning, a question I couldn't ignore: Is this enough?

This book is born from that question. It's the story of Amit, a character shaped by my observations, my experiences, and the shared struggles of countless individuals who have dared to ask if success, as we define it, truly satisfies the human soul. Amit's journey begins in the towering skyscrapers of Silicon Valley but unfolds in places far removed from the chaos—a tranquil mountain retreat, a humble village square, and within the silent recesses of his own mind.

The Duality of Laughter and Tears reflects the paradox of modern life. It speaks to the coexistence of joy and sorrow, connection and isolation, clarity and ambiguity. Amit's path is one of contrasts, where every triumph invites reflection and every challenge carries the seed of growth. Through his eyes, we explore the tension between the external chase for excellence and the internal quest for peace.

The subtitle, **Finding Silence in the Chaos of Silicon Valley**, encapsulates the heart of the narrative. Amid the unyielding hustle of a hyper-connected world, silence becomes a rare and transformative space. Amit's story is a reminder that stepping away isn't an escape; it's an act of courage. It's about pausing to listen to the whispers of our own hearts and finding meaning in moments we too often overlook.

This is not a guidebook or a prescription for a better life. It's an invitation—to reflect, to question, and to embrace the messiness of existence. The puzzle of life, as Amit discovers, isn't meant to be solved with certainty but lived with curiosity and courage. The duality we all navigate—laughter and tears, connection and solitude—is not a flaw but a testament to our shared humanity.

As you turn the pages, I hope Amit's journey resonates with you. May it encourage you to look beyond the noise, to celebrate both the highs and the lows, and to find your own silence in the chaos.

Welcome to *The Duality of Laughter and Tears*. May this story inspire you to live your questions fully, embrace the beauty of the incomplete, and discover the joy of simply being.

With gratitude,

Sandeep Chavan

Part I: Life—What a Puzzle

1: The Enigma Begins

Amit stood by the floor-to-ceiling window of his corner office, the San Francisco skyline stretching endlessly before him. The city's lights shimmered like a constellation brought to life, pulsating with the energy of millions chasing their ambitions. Tonight, those lights, usually a source of inspiration, felt oddly distant—like a puzzle he couldn't quite solve.

Behind him, the celebratory hum of the office party filled the air. Laughter mingled with the clinking of champagne glasses and the steady rhythm of congratulatory handshakes. The team at NeuroLink Innovations was basking in the glow of their latest triumph: the launch of *SynapseConnect*, a revolutionary neural interface. It was a technology that promised to seamlessly merge human thought with digital systems, heralding a new era of interaction between people and machines.

The accolades were pouring in—from investors, media outlets, and industry leaders. Yet, Amit felt a hollowness that the evening's triumph couldn't fill.

Seeking respite, he stepped onto the balcony, the cool night air wrapping around him. Below, the city pulsed with life, its streets alive with possibility. Amit pulled out his phone and dialed a familiar number.

It rang twice before his father's warm voice came through. "Amit, beta! Congratulations! I've been following the updates live."

Amit smiled, the genuine pride in his father's voice momentarily cutting through the unease. "Thanks, Papa. It's been a big night."

"I'm so proud of you," his father continued, his tone brimming with emotion. "Your mother is already telling everyone about her brilliant son. The neighbors probably know every detail of the launch by now."

Amit chuckled softly. "That sounds like Mom."

They spoke about the launch, the media buzz, and the promise of *SynapseConnect*. His father, ever curious, asked questions about its potential, listening intently as Amit described the technology's capabilities.

After a pause, his father's voice turned reflective. "Amit, may I ask you something?"

"Of course, Papa."

"This innovation you've created—it's remarkable, no doubt. But will it address the real struggles people face? Will it go beyond making life easier to actually improving it?"

The question landed like a quiet echo in Amit's mind, amplifying doubts he had long suppressed. "I... I suppose it will make things more efficient," he replied carefully. "Imagine controlling devices with just your thoughts or accessing information instantly."

His father's response was gentle but probing. "Efficiency is valuable, beta, but it's not everything. People are battling loneliness, stress, and a lack of purpose. Technology can solve problems, but it must serve humanity. Will *SynapseConnect* help people find what truly matters?"

Amit didn't have an answer. Staring out over the glittering expanse of the city, he murmured, "I hadn't thought about it that way."

"Your achievement is extraordinary," his father reassured him. "But remember, Amit, technology should uplift humanity, not just innovate for the sake of innovation."

The call ended soon after, but his father's words lingered. They illuminated a gap in Amit's vision, one he could no longer ignore.

A Seed of Doubt

Back inside, the party continued in full swing, but Amit moved through it with a growing sense of detachment. Colleagues congratulated him, investors applauded his vision, and yet all he could hear was his father's question: *Will it truly help people?*

Maya, his most trusted colleague and confidante, noticed the furrow in his brow. "You okay?" she asked, setting her glass down on a nearby table.

Amit nodded slowly. "I just spoke with my dad. He asked me a question that I can't get out of my head: Are we using this technology to truly help people, or are we just chasing innovation for its own sake?"

Maya's expression shifted from curiosity to contemplation. "That's... a big question for a party," she said with a faint smile.

"It is," Amit admitted. "But maybe it's the question I should've been asking all along. What if we've been so focused on impressing investors that we've lost sight of the bigger picture?"

Maya studied him for a moment. "If anyone can pivot this in a meaningful direction, it's you. We have the talent, the resources. Maybe it's time to think bigger."

"Not bigger," Amit corrected. "Deeper."

A Spark Ignites

For the remainder of the evening, Amit engaged his team in conversations about the potential of their work. He posed questions that were less about the next quarter's performance and more about the long-term impact of their innovations. To his surprise, many shared his desire to explore projects with a more profound social purpose.

By the time the party wound down, Amit's mind was racing with possibilities. Alone in his office, he pulled out a notebook and began sketching ideas: intuitive educational platforms for underserved communities, mental health tools powered by AI, interfaces designed for accessibility. Each idea felt like a step closer to aligning his work with a deeper purpose.

He sent a message to Maya: *"Let's schedule a meeting tomorrow. I have some ideas to discuss."*

Her reply came quickly: *"Looking forward to it."*

As the city lights began to blur into dawn, Amit stood once more at the window. He thought of his father's words and whispered, "Thank you, Papa." That single question had cracked open a door he hadn't realized was closed.

The Beginning of the Puzzle

The road ahead was veiled in uncertainty, its twists and turns hidden by the fog of possibility. Yet, for the first time in years, Amit felt something stir within him—a quiet but undeniable spark of purpose. It wasn't the kind of certainty

THE DUALITY OF LAUGHTER AND TEARS

he had once craved, but it was enough to illuminate the path ahead, even if only a few steps at a time.

Life, Amit realized, was not a problem to be solved with precision or a destination to be reached with haste. It was a puzzle—a beautifully chaotic, ever-evolving tapestry of moments, choices, and connections. Each piece held its own story, its own weight, and its own place. Some fit easily, slipping into position as if by magic, while others lingered on the edges, waiting for the right time to reveal their purpose. The beauty wasn't in completing the puzzle but in the act of engaging with it, piece by piece.

Standing by the window of his corner office, Amit watched the city awaken. The golden hues of the sunrise painted the skyline, casting long shadows over the labyrinth of streets below. What had once seemed like a battleground of competing ambitions now appeared as a living, breathing canvas—a network of lives, dreams, and stories intertwined in ways he was only beginning to understand.

The rhythms of the city no longer felt overwhelming; they felt alive, brimming with possibility. The honking of cars, the chatter of early risers, the distant hum of machinery—all of it seemed to harmonize, creating a symphony of human endeavor. Amit saw not the chaos of progress but the unity of purpose, a collective movement toward something greater than individual goals.

For so long, the unknown had been his greatest fear. It was the void he sought to fill with achievements, the shadow he tried to outpace with relentless ambition. But now, that same unknown inspired him. It was no longer a chasm to be avoided but a frontier to be explored, an invitation to live fully and courageously.

The enigma of purpose wasn't solved, and perhaps it never would be. But Amit was beginning to see that this was not a failure—it was a gift. The questions that once felt heavy now felt light, almost playful, like companions urging him forward. What if innovation wasn't about creating what was expected but about daring to reimagine what could be? What if success wasn't measured by accolades but by the impact left on the lives of others?

He was ready to live the questions, to embrace the uncertainty that had once paralyzed him. With every step, he would let curiosity guide him, trusting that the pieces of the puzzle would find their place in time. The work ahead wouldn't just be innovative; it would be meaningful. It would touch lives, bridge gaps, and create connections that outlasted fleeting trends and technologies.

Amit took a deep breath, feeling the cool morning air invigorate him. The world outside was alive with possibilities, and for the first time in a long while, he felt alive too. The puzzle of life stretched out before him—messy, incomplete, and utterly captivating.

This was no longer a journey to reach the end but a journey to find meaning in every step, to discover joy in the process, and to create a legacy not of perfection but of purpose. And that, Amit realized, was a puzzle worth solving.

2: Faces in the Crowd

The soft glow of chandeliers bathed the grand hall in a golden hue, illuminating the elegantly dressed guests. Laughter and lively conversations blended seamlessly with the mellow notes of a jazz quartet stationed in the corner. NeuroLink Innovations' celebration was in full swing, alive with the energy of success and anticipation.

Amit moved through the crowd, a polite smile fixed on his face. The conversation with his father lingered in his mind, its simplicity masking its depth. Clutching a glass of sparkling water, he exchanged pleasantries and accepted congratulations, but his heart wasn't entirely in it.

"Exceptional work, Amit!" exclaimed Mr. Thompson, a prominent investor whose face radiated enthusiasm. "This launch is just the beginning. We're on the cusp of something monumental."

"Thank you," Amit replied with practiced humility. "It's been a team effort."

As he continued mingling, Amit began to observe the spectrum of emotions around him. Genuine joy lit up the faces of some team members, their pride in the collective achievement evident. He noticed Maya laughing with a group of engineers, her enthusiasm so infectious it seemed to brighten the entire room. Her eyes sparkled with the kind of passion that came from truly believing in their work.

In contrast, other smiles felt forced, their wearers scanning the room for influential figures to impress. Amit spotted Mr. Harris, an executive from a competitor, feigning interest in a conversation while his gaze darted around, calculating his next move. The contrasts struck Amit deeply—the authenticity of some moments versus the hollow performativity of others.

He drifted toward the refreshment table, where Priya, a young intern, was balancing a plate of hors d'oeuvres. She brightened when she saw him.

"Congratulations, Amit! This is such an exciting time," she said earnestly.

"Thank you, Priya," he responded warmly. "Your work on the user interface has been a standout. It's been a big hit."

She blushed slightly. "I'm just grateful to be part of the team. It's inspiring to work on something that could make a real difference."

Her sincerity struck a chord. "Do you feel our work is making a difference?" he asked, genuinely curious.

"Absolutely," Priya replied without hesitation. "Imagine what SynapseConnect could mean for people with disabilities—those who struggle to communicate or perform everyday tasks. It's life-changing."

Amit nodded thoughtfully. Her words echoed the questions his father had asked earlier that evening. "You're right. The potential is incredible."

As Priya was called away by a colleague, Amit continued through the room, overhearing fragments of conversations:

"...market projections are off the charts..."

THE DUALITY OF LAUGHTER AND TEARS

"...think of the bonuses this quarter..."

"...I might finally get that vacation home..."

Amidst the celebration, Amit felt a growing sense of disconnect. For some, this was a moment to reflect on meaningful work; for others, it was merely a stepping stone to personal gain. The divergence in values was impossible to ignore.

In a quieter corner, he noticed Raj, a senior developer, standing alone, swirling a glass of wine as he stared into the distance. Amit approached him.

"Enjoying the party?" Amit asked.

Raj offered a faint smile. "It's quite an event. You really know how to celebrate success."

Amit chuckled softly. "The credit goes to the planning team. You seem deep in thought."

"Nights like this make me reflect," Raj admitted. "Why we do what we do, and whether it's enough."

"Care to share?" Amit encouraged.

Raj sighed. "I got into tech to create tools that could genuinely improve lives. Lately, I worry we're getting swept up in the race for innovation and losing sight of the human element."

Amit felt the weight of Raj's words. "I've been wrestling with the same thoughts. Do you think we've veered too far off course?"

"Sometimes," Raj replied. "But I also believe we can realign. It depends on leadership's willingness to prioritize impact over optics."

Amit nodded, the responsibility in Raj's statement settling on him. "What if we shifted focus to applications that address real-world problems? Mental health, accessibility, education—areas where we could make tangible differences."

Raj's expression brightened. "That would be incredible. We've barely scratched the surface of what we can do with this technology."

Their conversation was interrupted by boisterous laughter from a nearby group. Amit turned to see a cluster of executives engaged in exaggerated mirth, their display a stark contrast to the earnest dialogue he had been having. The duality of the evening struck him: authentic connections versus superficial interactions, joy intertwined with underlying tensions.

Later, he noticed Anika, a marketing manager, stepping out onto the terrace with a forced smile that quickly faded. Concerned, he followed her.

"Anika, is everything alright?" he asked gently.

She seemed startled but then relaxed. "Oh, Amit. I'm fine, just needed some air."

"Are you sure? You seemed upset," he pressed.

She sighed, leaning on the railing. "I should be happy—we've achieved so much. But my mother's health is declining, and I feel guilty being here instead of with her."

Amit's heart went out to her. "I'm sorry to hear that. If you need to take time off..."

"Thank you," she said, her eyes softening. "I didn't want to burden anyone tonight."

"You're not a burden," Amit assured her. "We're a team. Supporting each other is part of that."

As Anika returned inside, Amit remained on the terrace. The city stretched out before him, a tapestry of light and shadow. He reflected on the evening's contrasts—joy and

THE DUALITY OF LAUGHTER AND TEARS

sorrow, connection and isolation, success and doubt—all woven together in the fabric of life.

When he returned to the party, he sought out Maya. She was in the middle of an animated discussion but broke away when she saw him.

"You look like you've been philosophizing," she teased.

"I've been observing," Amit replied. "Noticing how happiness and challenges seem to coexist."

"That's life," Maya said. "A constant interplay of opposites."

"True happiness, I think, is learning to embrace that interplay," Amit mused. "The laughter and the tears."

Maya smiled. "It's a lesson worth fostering in our work too."

"Exactly," Amit agreed. "If we can create a culture that values people beyond productivity, we can inspire true fulfillment."

Maya's eyes brightened. "That's a vision I can get behind."

As the evening wound down, Amit gathered the remaining team members for a toast. "Tonight, we celebrate more than our achievements," he said, his voice steady. "We celebrate the journey—the highs, the lows, and the shared moments in between. Let's continue to innovate, but let's also build a culture where everyone feels valued for who they are."

Glasses clinked, and Amit felt a shared understanding ripple through the group. The night had been a reflection of life's complexities, and he was beginning to see the beauty in embracing them.

Walking out into the cool night, he breathed deeply. Life was a puzzle, its pieces ever-changing. But by acknowledging both joy and sorrow, he felt ready to face whatever lay ahead.

SANDEEP CHAVAN

Conclusion of Part I: Life—What a Puzzle

The city had settled into the quiet embrace of night as Amit stood alone on the rooftop terrace of his office building. The celebration had long since ended, the last guests bidding warm farewells and leaving behind echoes of laughter. Before him stretched the sprawling urban landscape, a glittering mosaic of lights mirrored by the constellations above. It was a stunning view, yet it felt less like a triumph and more like a riddle—an intricate puzzle that refused to offer easy answers.

Leaning against the cool metal railing, Amit let his thoughts unravel. The evening's events played in his mind: his father's probing words about the purpose of technology, Priya's youthful optimism about their work, Raj's candid reflections on meaning, and Anika's quiet struggle cloaked in a forced smile. Each interaction felt like a piece of a larger picture, fragments of clarity he was only beginning to piece together.

"Life truly is a puzzle," he murmured to himself. "An intricate mosaic of moments that don't always fit neatly together."

The duality of the night struck him deeply. Beneath the outward celebration of success lay currents of doubt, vulnerability, and longing. Laughter and tears had danced in parallel, revealing the complexity of the human experience. Amit began to realize that these opposing forces were not contradictions but complementary threads, each giving the other its depth and meaning.

His father's question lingered: *Will this technology help people come out of their regular life struggles?* It was deceptively

THE DUALITY OF LAUGHTER AND TEARS

simple but had struck at the heart of his journey. Amit had been so consumed by innovation and ambition that he hadn't fully considered the human impact of his work. The accolades and achievements suddenly felt hollow in comparison to the weight of that question.

He took a deep breath, the crisp night air filling his lungs and clearing his thoughts. The hum of the city below—the murmur of distant conversations, the occasional honk of a car, the faint hum of streetlights—became a reminder of the rhythm of life continuing unabated.

"Perhaps success isn't just about reaching the pinnacle," Amit thought. "Maybe it's about the journey and the connections we forge along the way."

He reflected on the faces he had seen in the crowd that evening. Each carried its own blend of joy and sorrow, victory and struggle. Some smiles were genuine, born from a sense of purpose; others were strained, thin veils over unspoken pain. Amit began to see that recognizing this duality in others was the first step toward embracing it within himself.

In that quiet moment, Amit made a silent vow: to align his work with a higher purpose, to create technology that truly addressed the struggles of people like the ones his father had described—the farmer battling hardship, the student longing for education, the elderly neighbor seeking connection. It was time to infuse his innovation with empathy and intention, to embrace life's complexities rather than shy away from them.

He thought about the people who had stood alongside him tonight: Maya's unwavering support, Priya's infectious optimism, Raj's yearning for deeper meaning, and Anika's silent courage. These individuals weren't just colleagues; they were fellow travelers, each navigating their own puzzles and enriching his in the process.

A soft breeze stirred, carrying with it a sense of peace. The uncertainty that had once felt burdensome now seemed like an open horizon, brimming with possibilities. Amit realized that solving life's puzzle didn't require having all the answers. It required openness, empathy, and the courage to face both light and shadow.

Descending from the rooftop, Amit walked through the quiet halls of his company. The sleek architecture, once a symbol of progress and innovation, now felt different—like a vessel ready to carry a vision rooted in humanity. He paused in the lobby, his gaze lingering on the vibrant mural of interconnected nodes and pathways. For the first time, it felt less like an abstract depiction of technology and more like a metaphor for the intricate web of human experiences.

Outside, the cool night air greeted him. The world seemed alive with potential, each moment an invitation to engage more deeply with the mysteries of existence. The interplay of laughter and tears no longer felt like opposing forces but as intertwined as the stars and city lights above.

As he made his way home, Amit felt a profound sense of gratitude. The questions that had once burdened him were now guiding lights, illuminating a path forward. Life's puzzle remained intricate and confounding at times, but he no longer feared its complexity.

He recalled a favorite quote of his father's: *"The mind is not a vessel to be filled but a fire to be kindled."* Amit felt that fire within him now—a flame fueled by curiosity, compassion, and a willingness to embrace all facets of life.

THE DUALITY OF LAUGHTER AND TEARS

Part I: *Life—What a Puzzle* had been a journey of awakening. Amit had begun to see beyond the surface of success, exploring the deeper layers of meaning and connection. The duality of laughter and tears had taught him that fulfillment wasn't a destination but a process—a continuous, imperfect, and beautiful engagement with life's intricacies.

As he reached his doorstep, Amit paused to take one last deep breath of the night air. Challenges and uncertainties awaited him, but they no longer felt daunting. Life's puzzle was far from complete, and it might never be. But for the first time, that incompleteness felt not like a flaw but a gift—a reminder to live fully, piece by imperfect piece.

With a quiet smile, Amit whispered to himself, "This is enough." And with that thought, he stepped inside, ready to embrace the next chapter.

Part II: The Mind's Slumber and the Chase for Dreams

3: The Lull

The soft hum of servers and distant murmurs of his team provided an unbroken backdrop as Amit sat in his office, bathed in the pale glow of multiple monitors. Lines of code and scrolling analytics reflected on his glasses, their constant motion mirroring the ceaseless churn of his thoughts. It was late—far later than he realized—but time had become an abstraction in the relentless race to meet deadlines.

He leaned back in his chair, rubbing his temples to ease the dull ache that had settled there. The impending launch of their latest update loomed large, its weight pressing down on him. Bugs to fix, investor reports to finalize, last-minute feature tweaks—the to-do list seemed infinite.

"Amit," Maya's voice cut through the silence. She stood in the doorway, her concern evident. "It's almost midnight. You need to get some rest."

Amit glanced at the clock, startled. "Is it that late already?"

She nodded, stepping inside with a takeaway container in hand. "I brought you dinner. I figured you'd forget to eat."

He offered a weary smile. "You're a lifesaver, Maya."

She set the container on his desk and sat opposite him. "Amit, when was the last time you truly took a break? And I don't mean a quick nap or a few hours away from your desk—I mean an actual break."

He waved off her concern. "After the launch. Right now, every moment counts."

She sighed, leaning forward. "You've been running on fumes for weeks. Even machines need downtime."

"I'll be fine," he assured her, his voice tinged with impatience.

Maya's expression softened, but her tone remained firm. "Just don't burn out. You're not doing anyone any favors if you crash."

As she left, Amit turned back to his screens, but her words lingered. He pushed through the night, his focus faltering as exhaustion blurred the lines of logic and productivity.

The next morning, as he entered the office with a fresh cup of coffee, Amit noticed a group of employees huddled together, their quiet conversation filled with subdued laughter. He greeted them, sensing an undercurrent of meaning in their exchange that eluded him.

"Everything okay?" he asked, trying to connect.

Raj, one of his senior developers, nodded. "Just talking about the weekend. It was… meaningful."

Amit felt a pang of disconnection. He couldn't even recall what day of the week it was. Offering a polite nod, he moved on, but the unsettled feeling gnawed at him.

Later, his phone buzzed during a meeting. Glancing at the screen, he saw a message from his sister, Anika: *Missed you at Dad's birthday yesterday. Everyone was asking about you.*

The words hit him like a freight train. He had forgotten his father's 60th birthday.

Excusing himself from the room, Amit dialed Anika, dread pooling in his stomach.

THE DUALITY OF LAUGHTER AND TEARS

"Amit," she answered, her voice laced with irritation.

"Anika, I'm so sorry. I lost track of time," he began, his words tumbling out.

She sighed. "Do you realize how important this was to him? To all of us? We had a video call set up for you."

"I know. I have no excuse," he admitted. "How is Dad?"

"He's disappointed. He won't say it, but we can all tell."

Amit's guilt deepened. "I'll call him right now."

"Please do," she urged. "And, Amit... think about what really matters."

He hesitated for a moment before dialing his father's number.

"Amit, beta! How are you?" his father greeted him warmly, masking any hurt.

"Happy belated birthday, Papa. I'm so sorry I missed it," Amit said earnestly.

"It's alright," his father replied gently. "I know you're busy."

"No, it's not alright," Amit countered. "I should have been there. I let work take over everything."

His father paused. "We missed you. But perhaps this is life's way of reminding you to slow down. You've been running so fast you've forgotten to look around."

The words struck a chord deep within Amit. He realized how disconnected he had become from his family, his values, and even himself.

After ending the call, he sat at his desk, his monitors now seeming like lifeless rectangles of glass and metal. Maya's earlier warning echoed in his mind.

She appeared at his door again, sensing his turmoil. "You okay?"

"I missed my father's birthday," he admitted.

Her expression softened. "I'm sorry, Amit."

"I've been so absorbed in work that I've stopped living. I've been running on autopilot," he said, his voice heavy with self-reproach.

"Then take a break," Maya urged. "Reconnect. The team can handle things for a few days."

It was daunting, but Amit knew she was right. That evening, he booked a flight home.

As he walked through the bustling streets of Mumbai the next day, memories of his childhood mingled with a bittersweet nostalgia. At the airport, his father greeted him with an embrace that spoke volumes.

"Welcome home, beta."

"It's good to be here," Amit replied, a lump in his throat.

Over the next few days, Amit immersed himself in family life. He cooked with his mother, reminisced with his sister, and joined his father at the community center where he volunteered. These moments were simple but profound, each one peeling back the layers of detachment Amit had built around himself.

One evening, as he sat on the balcony with his father, they watched the city lights together.

"You seem lighter," his father observed.

"I feel awake for the first time in years," Amit admitted. "Like I've been chasing something without understanding why."

His father nodded. "Awareness is the first step. Now, you can choose what matters most."

THE DUALITY OF LAUGHTER AND TEARS

Back at work, Amit carried this renewed perspective with him. He proposed initiatives to focus on technology that addressed real-world issues—education, healthcare, and accessibility. The team, inspired by his clarity, rallied behind the vision.

Amit realized that the lull he had experienced wasn't just a pause; it was an awakening. He had been forced to confront the disconnect in his life, and in doing so, he found a path toward integration.

Philosophical Reflection

Amit's journey in this chapter serves as a poignant illustration of the quiet dangers of a life lived on autopilot—a life where relentless ambition narrows our focus to achievements, often at the expense of the very things that give those achievements meaning. It's not just the missed birthday that stands out as a symbol of disconnection but the emotional distance it represents. That forgotten moment is a microcosm of a larger detachment from relationships, self-awareness, and the richness of life itself.

The rhythm of modern ambition often sweeps us along, convincing us that each success will bring the satisfaction we crave. But as Amit realizes, the milestones he so rigorously pursued had become hollow markers, devoid of the warmth of connection or the joy of shared experience. His missed commitments, once brushed aside as minor sacrifices for the greater good, come into sharp focus as symptoms of a deeper imbalance—a life that values doing over being.

The experience becomes Amit's wake-up call, a quiet but profound moment of reckoning. In the stillness of his realization, he begins to confront the priorities that have guided him. What has he truly gained if the successes he celebrates are experienced in isolation? What has he lost in the relentless pursuit of a future he can never fully predict? These questions, though uncomfortable, open a door to transformation.

Amit's reflection is not just personal but universally resonant. It calls into question a cultural narrative that equates relentless striving with fulfillment and equates presence with passivity. The narrative suggests an alternative path, one where

THE DUALITY OF LAUGHTER AND TEARS

ambition is not abandoned but harmonized with purpose, presence, and meaningful relationships. Amit begins to see that fulfillment is not a distant destination but something cultivated in the choices we make every day—in the connections we nurture, in the time we give, and in the simple, profound act of showing up fully for our lives.

His awakening becomes a reminder of the impermanence of moments and the irreplaceable value of living them with intention. It's not enough to achieve; one must also pause to appreciate, reflect, and realign. Life, Amit learns, is not a race to a finish line but a journey to be experienced with open eyes and an open heart.

In embracing this perspective, Amit begins to rediscover a sense of harmony. He learns that success is not measured by accolades or titles but by the depth of his presence and the authenticity of his connections. He starts to reclaim the beauty of the ordinary—the laughter shared over a meal, the quiet of a sunset, the warmth of a genuine conversation. These are the moments that give life its complexity and meaning, far beyond the fleeting satisfaction of professional triumphs.

Amit's story is an invitation to all of us. It urges us to step off the treadmill of relentless striving, even briefly, to ask ourselves: What are we pursuing, and at what cost? Are we awake to the beauty of the present, or are we too preoccupied with a future that may never come as we imagine? It is a universal reminder to pause, reflect, and live with intention—to find harmony between ambition and presence, and to measure success not by what we achieve but by how we live and whom we touch along the way.

SANDEEP CHAVAN

In Amit's reckoning, we find our own—a call to awaken, to realign, and to embrace life in all its fleeting, imperfect, and extraordinary wonder.

4: Chasing Shadows

The morning sun seeped through the blinds of Amit's office, painting striped patterns across a desk cluttered with notebooks, sketches, and a half-empty mug of coffee long gone cold. The faint chatter of the office faded into the background as Amit's gaze remained fixed on his laptop, where lines of code and schematic designs blurred together. His thoughts raced faster than his fingers could type, driven by an urgency that felt both exhilarating and suffocating.

Since returning from his family visit, Amit had been consumed by a sense of purpose. The time at home had reignited his conviction to create meaningful change, and he believed he had found the answer in *Lumina*—a groundbreaking project aimed at developing affordable, smart devices for underserved communities.

"*Lumina* will change everything," he thought as his fingers flew across the keyboard. "It'll bridge the gap, bringing technology to those left behind."

The enthusiasm was contagious, at first. The team rallied behind the vision, their excitement palpable during brainstorming sessions. They dreamed of solar-powered devices with intuitive interfaces that could provide educational content, healthcare information, and reliable connectivity to remote villages. Amit's eyes sparkled as he described the possibilities.

"Imagine a farmer receiving real-time weather updates to save their crops," he told his team. "Or a child in a rural school accessing the same quality education as anyone in the city."

But as weeks turned into months, the cracks began to show. Technical challenges emerged—battery life limitations, high manufacturing costs, unreliable network infrastructure. Each new obstacle seemed to fuel Amit's obsession, as though sheer determination could bend reality to his will.

"We just need to work harder," he insisted during one late-night meeting. "If we can solve these issues, think of the difference we'll make."

Maya, seated across the table, exchanged weary glances with the rest of the team. "Amit, the team is exhausted. Maybe we need to reassess our approach."

"There's no time to slow down," he countered, his tone resolute. "We're on the brink of something extraordinary."

"At what cost?" Maya pressed gently. "People are burning out. *You're* burning out."

"This is bigger than us," Amit shot back, his voice rising. "Great achievements require sacrifice."

The Obsession Deepens

Determined to push through, Amit began shouldering more responsibilities himself. He buried himself in technical manuals, learned new programming languages, and coordinated with suppliers across time zones. Sleep became a luxury, meals an afterthought. The vision of *Lumina* consumed him, leaving little room for anything—or anyone—else.

THE DUALITY OF LAUGHTER AND TEARS

Late one evening, Raj knocked hesitantly on Amit's office door.

"What is it, Raj?" Amit asked, not looking up.

"We're hitting walls with the hardware specs," Raj said cautiously. "The components we need are driving up costs beyond what's feasible."

"Then find alternatives," Amit replied curtly.

"We've tried," Raj persisted. "Maybe we should consider scaling back some features."

"Absolutely not," Amit snapped. "Compromising now would undermine everything we're trying to achieve."

Raj sighed, his frustration evident. "Amit, we all believe in *Lumina*, but we need to be realistic. If we keep pushing like this, we risk destabilizing the entire company."

Amit's gaze hardened. "Do you believe in this project or not?"

"I do," Raj said, exasperated. "But belief alone won't solve these problems."

As Raj left, Amit's inflexibility became the talk of the office. Morale plummeted, and quiet grumblings filled the hallways. Maya, watching the strain ripple through the team, decided to confront him.

"You're pushing everyone, including yourself, too hard," she said one evening.

"I've told you," Amit said, barely glancing up. "Great achievements require effort."

"At this rate, all you'll achieve is burnout," Maya countered. "You're chasing shadows, Amit."

He frowned. "What's that supposed to mean?"

"It means you're pursuing an idealized vision without grounding it in reality," she explained. "You're so fixated on the destination that you're losing sight of the journey."

Amit bristled. "I thought you understood. This isn't just about a product—it's about making a difference."

"And I believe in that," she replied, her tone calm but firm. "But even the best intentions need a sustainable path forward. Dreams without balance are nothing more than illusions."

A Turning Point

That night, Amit sat alone in the office. The silence, once a source of focus, now felt oppressive. He glanced around at the empty desks and the blinking cursor on his screen. A calendar reminder popped up—a charity gala he had promised to attend weeks ago.

The gala was hosted by an organization that supported educational initiatives in underserved communities—the very cause that had inspired *Lumina*. Amit dismissed the notification but hesitated. In his obsession with the project, he had isolated himself not only from his team but also from the broader impact he claimed to champion.

The next morning, Amit called an all-hands meeting. The team gathered with trepidation, unsure of what to expect.

"Thank you all for coming," Amit began, his voice uncharacteristically subdued. "I owe you all an apology. In my determination to make *Lumina* a reality, I've pushed too hard and ignored the toll it's taken on all of us."

Surprised murmurs rippled through the room.

"I lost sight of the fact that no project—no matter how noble—is worth compromising our health and well-being," he continued. "Effective immediately, we'll pause and reevaluate our approach. I want us to pursue this dream together, not at the expense of ourselves."

A tentative optimism replaced the tension. Maya stepped forward, offering a rare smile. "Thank you, Amit. That means a lot."

Raj raised his hand. "We all want to see *Lumina* succeed. If we approach it in phases, I think we can make it work."

Embracing Balance

In the weeks that followed, the team reorganized. They broke *Lumina* into smaller, manageable phases with realistic goals. Work-life balance initiatives were introduced, and Amit made a conscious effort to reconnect with his team, seeking their input and genuinely listening to their concerns.

As progress resumed at a sustainable pace, Amit realized that chasing an elusive ideal had blinded him to the importance of the process. Dreams, he understood now, were not meant to be pursued at all costs but cultivated with care and collaboration.

Sitting in the office one afternoon, reviewing the revised project plan, Amit felt a sense of calm he hadn't experienced in months. The shadows he had once pursued had given way to tangible progress, grounded in shared purpose and mutual respect.

He caught Maya's eye across the room, and she nodded approvingly. For the first time, Amit felt not just like a leader, but like part of a team united by a common goal.

Because in the end, he realized, life—and work—isn't about relentless pursuit. It's about finding meaning in the journey, cherishing the people who walk alongside you, and grounding your dreams in the reality of the present moment.

5: The Dreamer's Dilemma

The morning mist hung low over the lake in the city park, blurring the line between water and sky. Amit stood at the edge of the tranquil scene, his thoughts as still and restless as the world around him. He had taken to visiting this park in the early hours, seeking clarity in the serenity of dawn. The quiet offered a reprieve from the ceaseless demands of his office, the buzzing world of deadlines and expectations left behind.

Yet, as the ripples on the lake mirrored the faint stirrings of the wind, Amit felt unsettled. Despite the recent course corrections at work and the team's renewed energy, he couldn't shake the unease that had settled within him. The excitement that once fueled his pursuit of *Lumina* had dimmed, replaced by a gnawing sense of incompleteness. Was he truly on the right path? Or was he simply chasing an ever-moving horizon, further from fulfillment with every step?

Lost in thought, he didn't notice the elderly man approaching until he spoke.

"Beautiful morning, isn't it?"

Amit turned to find a dignified figure standing beside him. The man, in his seventies, leaned lightly on a walking stick. His silver hair and warm smile radiated a calm wisdom.

"Yes," Amit replied, offering a faint smile. "It's peaceful."

THE DUALITY OF LAUGHTER AND TEARS

The two stood in silence, watching as the mist began to lift, revealing the shimmering surface of the lake.

"Do you come here often?" the man asked.

"Lately, yes," Amit admitted. "It helps me think."

"Ah, a seeker of clarity," the man said with a knowing nod. "I'm Ravi."

"Amit," he replied, extending his hand.

"Pleasure to meet you, Amit."

Ravi leaned on his stick, gazing thoughtfully at the lake. "Stillness has a way of revealing what motion often conceals."

Amit was struck by the depth of the observation. "Are you a philosopher?" he asked lightly, trying to mask his curiosity.

Ravi chuckled. "In a way. I've spent my life exploring questions rather than chasing answers."

"What kind of questions?"

"The big ones," Ravi said, his eyes twinkling. "Purpose, happiness, success. Questions that don't have easy answers."

Amit felt drawn to Ravi's presence, as though the man had been placed there at precisely the right moment. "Those are questions I've been struggling with too."

"Then perhaps we've met for a reason," Ravi said. "What's on your mind?"

Amit hesitated but found himself opening up. "I've been chasing this vision—to create something meaningful, something that changes lives. But the closer I get, the more it feels... hollow. Like contentment is always just out of reach."

Ravi listened intently. "And what do you think is holding contentment back?"

Amit sighed. "I'm not sure. I thought if I worked hard enough, if I poured everything into my dreams, I'd find it. But now, I'm not so certain."

"Sometimes," Ravi said, his voice gentle, "we chase grand dreams, hoping they'll fill the void within us. But in doing so, we often overlook the simpler joys that bring true happiness."

"What do you mean?"

"Tell me," Ravi asked, "what brings you joy outside of your work?"

Amit paused, searching for an answer. "Moments like this. Time with family. Conversations with friends."

"And how much time do you devote to those things?"

Amit's shoulders sagged. "Not enough. Work always comes first."

"It's a common dilemma," Ravi said with a small smile. "We believe ambition will lead us to fulfillment, but often, it leads us away from the very things that give life meaning."

Amit frowned. "But isn't it important to have dreams? To strive for something greater?"

"Of course," Ravi agreed. "Dreams inspire us, drive innovation, give life purpose. But the question is: at what cost? If the pursuit of those dreams consumes you to the point of losing yourself, is the sacrifice worth it?"

The question lingered in the air, as expansive as the lake before them.

"How do you find the balance?" Amit asked finally. "How do you pursue your dreams without losing yourself?"

"It's not easy," Ravi admitted. "It requires introspection and honesty. You must ask yourself why you're chasing these

THE DUALITY OF LAUGHTER AND TEARS

dreams. Is it for validation? Ego? Or is it to genuinely contribute to the world?"

"I'd like to think it's the latter," Amit said, though doubt tinged his voice.

"Then it's a matter of redefining success," Ravi said. "True success isn't a relentless climb to an ever-shifting summit. It's in the impact you make, the relationships you nurture, the growth you experience along the way."

Amit was quiet for a moment, gazing at the ripples spreading across the water. "But doesn't slowing down mean falling behind?"

"Not at all," Ravi replied. "Slowing down doesn't mean you're giving up. It means you're creating space—to breathe, to reflect, to reconnect with what truly matters."

The words struck Amit like a key turning in a lock.

"May I share a story?" Ravi asked.

"Please," Amit said, eager to listen.

Ravi began to recount his younger days—building a thriving business, achieving financial success, but at the cost of his health and relationships. "I lost someone very dear to me," Ravi said, his voice softening. "That loss forced me to see how much I'd sacrificed in my pursuit of success."

"What did you do?"

"I stepped back," Ravi said. "I entrusted my business to capable hands and focused on reconnecting—with myself, with loved ones, with life. I found fulfillment in simplicity."

"Do you regret stepping back?"

"Not for a moment," Ravi said with conviction. "Ambition and contentment aren't enemies. They can coexist if you align your pursuits with your values."

The conversation stretched into the morning, each exchange a layer peeled back from Amit's own questions. When they parted, Ravi left him with a simple yet profound thought:

"Success is not the destination, Amit. It's how you walk the journey."

A Shift in Perspective

Back at the office, Amit approached his day differently. He paused before diving into tasks, taking a moment to consider his intentions. He began to see his team not just as colleagues but as people with their own dreams and struggles.

In a meeting with Maya and Raj, he shared his reflections. "We need to redefine success," he said. "Not just in terms of products or profits, but in how we live and work together."

Maya looked at him, surprised but intrigued. "That's a big shift, Amit."

"It's a necessary one," he said. "If we can find balance and stay true to our values, we can achieve something far greater than just innovation."

Weeks passed, and the workplace began to change. Amit noticed the difference within himself as well. He felt more present, more at peace. The dreams he once chased relentlessly no longer felt like distant shadows but like guiding lights he could approach with grace.

One afternoon, a text lit up his phone: "Trust your inner voice. All the best. – Ravi."

Amit smiled, feeling a sense of gratitude for the encounter that had altered his path.

As the sun dipped below the horizon, casting the city in hues of orange and pink, Amit stood by the window, reflecting.

THE DUALITY OF LAUGHTER AND TEARS

The dreamer's dilemma was no longer a question of whether to chase or to pause. It was about finding harmony—pursuing dreams with an open heart, grounded in the richness of the present moment.

And as he gazed out at the cityscape, Amit knew he was no longer running. He was walking, step by step, toward a vision that felt not just achievable but truly worthwhile.

Conclusion of Part II: The Mind's Slumber and the Chase for Dreams

The evening sky was awash with hues of deep indigo and soft violet as Amit sat on a quiet bench overlooking the lake in the city park. The gentle ripples on the water's surface mirrored the subtle stirrings of his mind. Days of introspection and revelation had led him to this tranquil moment, a pause amidst the whirlwind of his life's recent chapters.

He reflected on his journey—a labyrinth of ambitions, achievements, and anxieties. It had been all too easy for his mind to slip into complacency, lulled by the familiar rhythms of routine and the seductive allure of unchecked ambition. Operating on autopilot, he had allowed his days to blur together, each one a mere echo of the last. The stark wake-up call of missing his father's milestone birthday had jolted him from this unconscious drift, forcing him to confront the shadows he'd been chasing.

Determined to realign his life, Amit sought to reconnect—with his family, his colleagues, and most importantly, with himself. Yet, even as he endeavored to adjust his course, old patterns beckoned. The creation of *Lumina* became a new obsession, a dream he pursued with relentless fervor, convinced it held the key to his fulfillment.

But the harder he chased this elusive ideal, the further it seemed to slip away, leading him deeper into a maze of exhaustion and strained relationships. His mind, though awakened from complacency, became ensnared in the ceaseless pursuit of an ever-shifting goal. The vision that once inspired

THE DUALITY OF LAUGHTER AND TEARS

him now cast long shadows, obscuring the very values he sought to uphold.

It was a chance encounter with Ravi—the wise, contemplative man by the lake—that offered Amit a lifeline back to clarity. Ravi's gentle questions and profound insights challenged him to examine the true nature of his aspirations. Was he chasing dreams that resonated with his authentic self, or was he driven by external validations and a fear of standing still? Ravi's story of personal loss and the redefinition of success served as a mirror, reflecting the potential consequences of a life out of balance.

Amit realized that while dreams are vital—they inspire growth and innovation—the pursuit becomes hollow when it leads us away from inner peace and genuine happiness. The mind's tendency to fixate on distant horizons can blind us to the beauty and fulfillment available in the present moment. He understood now that contentment is not the enemy of ambition but its companion, guiding it with purpose and mindfulness.

As stars began to punctuate the twilight sky, Amit felt a profound sense of acceptance wash over him. He acknowledged the dual nature of his journey—the necessity of dreams to propel us forward and the importance of staying grounded to appreciate the path we walk. The mind must be both awake to the present and open to the future, navigating the delicate balance between aspiration and contentment.

He thought of the themes that had woven through this chapter of his life:

- **The Mind's Slumber:** The danger of falling into

complacency, allowing routine and unexamined ambition to dull our awareness of what truly matters.
- **Chasing Shadows:** The realization that relentless pursuit without mindfulness can lead us away from happiness, as we become consumed by goals that may not align with our authentic selves.

Rising from the bench, Amit felt lighter yet more grounded than he had in a long time. The cool evening air carried the scent of blooming jasmine, a subtle reminder of life's simple pleasures. He made a silent commitment to embrace his dreams with a conscious mind and an open heart, ensuring that each step he took was in harmony with his values and well-being.

Returning to his life and work, Amit sought to foster a culture that valued balance, presence, and genuine fulfillment. He encouraged his team to pursue innovation not just for its own sake but as a means to enrich their lives and the lives of others meaningfully. Together, they began to redefine success—not as a distant destination to be frantically reached but as a journey to be savored and shared.

He initiated open dialogues within his team, inviting them to express their own aspirations and concerns. Work-life balance became a priority, with flexible schedules and opportunities for personal growth outside the office. Amit also rekindled his involvement with community projects, understanding that giving back was a vital component of a fulfilling life.

THE DUALITY OF LAUGHTER AND TEARS

One evening, as he stood by his office window overlooking the city, Maya joined him. The skyline shimmered with a million lights, each one representing a unique story.

"You seem different," she observed, a soft smile playing on her lips.

"I feel different," Amit replied. "I've realized that chasing dreams shouldn't mean running ourselves into the ground."

She nodded thoughtfully. "It's about the journey, isn't it?"

"Exactly," he agreed. "And making sure that journey enriches us and those around us."

Maya looked at him, her eyes reflecting the city's glow. "I'm glad you're finding your path."

Amit smiled. "Me too."

As he walked home that night, the gentle rustling of leaves accompanied his footsteps. The night sky above was vast and open, mirroring the possibilities that lay before him—a canvas upon which he could paint a life of balanced ambition and true contentment.

He understood now that awakening the mind from complacency is only the first step; guiding it wisely is the ongoing journey. By questioning the paths we tread and the dreams we chase, we open ourselves to a more authentic and fulfilling existence. Amit felt ready to embrace whatever came next, knowing that he carried within him the tools to navigate both triumphs and trials.

Because in aligning our dreams with our deepest values, we find not only the path to success but also the way to inner peace.

Part III: Beyond Dreams

6: The Turning Point

Amit sat in his office, his fingers hovering over the keyboard, paralyzed by indecision. The pale glow of his monitor illuminated his face, casting shadows that deepened the lines etched by months of relentless work. The charts and projections on the screen—markers of *Lumina's* progress—blurred together, mocking his inability to focus. Once a source of pride and inspiration, these symbols of his ambition now felt hollow, as if stripped of the meaning they once carried.

The steady hum of the air conditioning filled the room, punctuated by the occasional rustle of papers on his desk. Outside, the city pulsed with life—sirens wailed in the distance, cars honked along crowded streets, and muffled voices floated up from the streets below. But within these four walls, Amit was enveloped in a stillness that felt suffocating, a vacuum of purpose that no amount of busyness could dispel.

He leaned back, staring blankly at the ceiling, his mind numb and devoid of its usual spark. This wasn't just exhaustion; it was a deeper malaise. A gnawing sense of disconnection crept into every thought, a shadow he couldn't ignore. *Lumina,* the project that had once ignited his soul, now felt like a machine running on momentum alone, its original spark dimmed by the relentless grind.

His phone buzzed on the desk, breaking the oppressive silence. Amit glanced at the screen: a message from his sister, Anika. The short message carried an urgency that made his chest tighten:

"Call me. It's important."

He dialed her number immediately. Anika answered on the first ring, her voice tight with worry.

"Amit," she began, her tone carrying the weight of bad news.

"What's wrong?" he asked, trying to steady his voice despite the rising dread.

"It's Papa," she replied. "He had chest pain this morning. We're at the hospital now."

Her words hit him like a blow. "What? Chest pain? Is he okay? What did the doctors say?"

"They're running tests," Anika said quickly. "They think it might have been a mild heart attack. He's stable for now, but he's asking for you."

Amit felt the room tilt slightly, his grip on the phone tightening. "I'll book the next flight. Tell him I'm coming."

Anika exhaled audibly, her relief evident. "Please hurry, Amit."

As he hung up, the weight of the news pressed down on him. For a long moment, he sat frozen, his mind replaying memories of his father—his steady presence, his calming words during difficult times, his unshakable belief in Amit's potential. But alongside those memories came a sharp pang of regret. How often had he taken that presence for granted? How many calls had he rushed through, too preoccupied with work to linger?

THE DUALITY OF LAUGHTER AND TEARS

His gaze fell on his desk, cluttered with prototypes, notes, and financial reports. It was a monument to his ambition, but also a stark reminder of what he had neglected. His relentless pursuit of *Lumina* had come at a cost—missed dinners, canceled visits, and the steady erosion of time with the people who mattered most.

The screech of his chair against the floor broke the silence as he stood abruptly. He grabbed his coat and bag, ignoring the surprised glances of his team still working late into the night. At home, he hastily packed a suitcase, his hands trembling as memories of family dinners, his father's laughter, and moments of quiet counsel swirled in his mind.

At the airport, Amit moved through the motions of check-in and security in a daze. The bustle of travelers, the crackling announcements, and the mechanical hum of the terminal blurred into background noise. As the plane took off, he stared out at the receding city lights, his thoughts a maelstrom of fear and regret.

The realization hit him like a tidal wave: for all his ambition, for all the accolades and progress he had achieved, he had been climbing a mountain without stopping to appreciate the view—or the people cheering him on from below. *What was it all worth if it came at the cost of relationships, of love, of presence?*

At the hospital, the sterile scent of disinfectant and the rhythmic beep of monitors greeted him as he hurried through the corridors. He spotted Anika outside their father's room, her face pale but calm.

"He's stable now," she reassured him. "The doctors say it was mild, but he needs rest."

Relief flooded him as he stepped into the room. His father lay against the stark white sheets, frail yet smiling as Amit approached.

"Beta," his father greeted softly, his voice warm despite its fragility. "You came."

Amit's throat tightened as he took his father's hand. "Of course, Papa. I'm so sorry I wasn't here sooner."

His father shook his head. "You're here now. That's what matters."

In those few words, Amit felt the weight of time and regret dissipate slightly. The simplicity of his father's statement carried a profound truth: it wasn't too late to reconnect, to realign his priorities, to be present.

Over the next few days, Amit found a rhythm in the hospital. He stayed by his father's side, helped him with meals, and took careful notes during the doctors' updates. He watched as families in the waiting areas shared quiet moments of solidarity, their hushed conversations and comforting gestures a testament to life's interconnectedness.

One evening, as his father dozed, Amit spoke softly. "Papa, I've been thinking a lot. I've been so focused on building something impactful that I've lost sight of the people and moments that really matter."

His father opened his eyes, his gaze steady and knowing. "Ambition is important, beta," he said. "But life isn't just about achievements. It's about the people you share it with."

The turning point wasn't a grand epiphany, but a gradual awakening. It came in the form of small moments: the warmth of his mother's voice as she reminisced about their childhood, the laughter of his niece and nephew over ice cream, the quiet

THE DUALITY OF LAUGHTER AND TEARS

strength of Anika as she managed the household with grace. Amit realized that these moments—these simple, ordinary experiences—were the essence of life.

On his last night in Mumbai, Amit sat with his father in the garden, the scent of jasmine filling the air. His father's words lingered long after the evening breeze carried them away: "Life is a journey, beta, not a race. Take time to enjoy the view."

Back in the city, Amit carried the wisdom of those days with him. He approached work differently, calling a meeting with his leadership team to propose changes: flexible schedules, mental health resources, and a renewed focus on meaningful, impactful projects. He emphasized that success wasn't just about results but about fostering a culture of balance and fulfillment.

For the first time in years, Amit felt aligned—not just with his work but with his values. His father's words remained a guiding light, reminding him that true success wasn't in the chase but in the moments he chose to cherish along the way.

As he looked out over the city one evening, the skyline shimmering with life, Amit smiled. He wasn't just building a career; he was building a life—a life that balanced ambition with connection, achievement with presence, and dreams with the joy of simply being.

7: Into the Unknown

Amit stood on the balcony of his apartment, gazing at the sprawling cityscape one last time. The familiar twinkling lights, once a symbol of ambition and possibility, now seemed like a distant echo of a life he had outgrown. He sipped his coffee slowly, the warm bitterness grounding him as a swirl of emotions churned within—excitement, apprehension, and an unmistakable sense of liberation.

The decision to leave *Lumina* had not come easily. It had been a process marked by sleepless nights, endless pros-and-cons lists, and heartfelt conversations with family and close friends. Yet, the clarity to take this leap came not in moments of noise but in stillness—during a solitary early morning run in the park, as the sun's golden rays broke over the horizon. In that quiet moment, a voice within him urged, *It's time.*

For years, Amit had been chasing milestones, climbing ladders, and building what many would call a dream life. Yet, the glitter of his success had always veiled a persistent void. Now, standing at the edge of change, he felt ready to step into the unknown, carrying with him the lessons he had learned and the man he was becoming.

The farewell party at *Lumina* was a bittersweet gathering. It took place in the sunlit atrium where Amit and his team had

THE DUALITY OF LAUGHTER AND TEARS

once brainstormed ideas, celebrated milestones, and weathered challenges together. The space, decorated with colorful streamers and balloons, bore witness to the complex emotions that filled the room—joy, nostalgia, and the quiet sadness of goodbyes.

Maya and Raj had orchestrated every detail. Laughter echoed as colleagues shared stories, while a slideshow of photos brought both smiles and tears. At the center of it all was a large cake with the words: *"To New Beginnings – Thank You, Amit!"*

Maya, holding a champagne flute, tapped it lightly with a spoon. The room hushed, and all eyes turned to her as she began her toast. "I'll admit," she started, her playful smirk softening the tension, "I didn't think you'd actually go through with it." Laughter rippled through the crowd. Then her tone shifted, becoming more sincere. "But Amit, I respect your courage. It's not easy to step away from something you've poured so much of yourself into. *Lumina* wouldn't be what it is today without your vision, your determination, and your relentless drive."

Raising her glass higher, she continued, "Here's to Amit—not just a leader, but a mentor, a friend, and an inspiration. May your next chapter be as impactful as the legacy you've left here."

Applause erupted, filling the room with an energy that was equal parts celebration and farewell. Amit smiled warmly, though his eyes reflected the weight of the moment. He looked around at the faces that had become like family—each one a reminder of shared triumphs, challenges, and camaraderie.

When it was his turn to speak, Amit stood slowly, taking a deep breath to steady himself. "Thank you, Maya," he began, his voice steady but thick with emotion. "And thank you to all of you—for being part of this incredible journey. Together, we've built something remarkable. And while I'm stepping away, I'll carry the memories of our time together with me always."

He paused, letting his gaze travel across the room. "But sometimes," he continued, "we have to step away from what's familiar to discover what truly fulfills us. For me, this isn't an ending—it's a beginning. I don't know exactly what's ahead, and yes, that's a little terrifying. But it's also exciting. And I'm ready to find out."

The applause that followed was softer, more profound, as if each clap carried an unspoken wish for his success. Later, as the night wound down, the conversations grew quieter, filled with earnest goodbyes and words of encouragement. Maya handed Amit a small envelope. "For when you need a reminder," she said with a smile, her voice tinged with emotion. He slipped it into his pocket, silently promising to open it when the time was right.

A week later, Amit found himself standing at the edge of a small village nestled in the foothills of the Himalayas. The crisp air carried the scent of pine and damp earth, mingling with the faint murmur of a stream. The terraced fields, simple stone houses, and winding dirt paths painted a picture of timeless simplicity. It was as if he had stepped into a world unburdened by the frenetic pace of modern life.

Each morning, Amit woke to the soft light of dawn spilling through wooden shutters. Wrapped in a shawl, he would step outside to watch the sunrise, the golden rays illuminating the mist that clung to the valleys. The beauty of those moments, untouched and eternal, filled him with a quiet awe.

THE DUALITY OF LAUGHTER AND TEARS

His days were spent in rhythm with the villagers. He joined them in harvesting crops, tending livestock, and repairing homes. At first, his clumsy attempts drew laughter, but his sincerity earned their trust. The work was hard, yet it brought a sense of accomplishment unlike anything he had felt in years. In the evenings, he sat around a crackling fire, listening to stories woven with humor and wisdom, their universal truths resonating deeply.

One evening, Amit found himself in a clearing overlooking snow-capped peaks, his notebook resting on his lap. The stillness around him mirrored the newfound calm within. He wrote freely, capturing fragments of clarity and questions that still lingered. In those pages, he articulated a realization: *I am not defined by my achievements. My worth lies in my ability to love, to connect, and to find joy in the simple act of being.*

The words felt like a revelation, distilling the essence of his journey thus far. For years, Amit had measured his life by external markers of success, chasing goals that never truly satisfied. Now, amidst the hills and simplicity of village life, he was beginning to uncover a deeper truth: fulfillment wasn't something to achieve—it was something to live.

The opportunity to trek to a remote monastery came unexpectedly, mentioned by a fellow traveler at the village market. Intrigued, Amit decided to join. The journey was grueling, the trail demanding every ounce of physical and mental strength. Yet, the breathtaking beauty of the landscape and the camaraderie of his fellow travelers made each step worthwhile.

Reaching the monastery, perched precariously on a cliff's edge, was like stepping into another world. The monks, serene and welcoming, embodied a quiet wisdom that left Amit in awe. Their simple lives, rooted in purpose and mindfulness, offered a stark contrast to the complexity he had left behind.

Through shared meals, meditations, and conversations, Amit learned lessons that felt both ancient and immediate. One monk's words lingered with him: *"Life is not a problem to be solved but a mystery to be lived."* It was a reminder that fulfillment wasn't found in answers but in the courage to embrace uncertainty.

Returning to the village, Amit felt a profound shift within himself. The unknown, once a source of fear, had become a space of possibility. The lessons he had learned—about presence, connection, and purpose—reshaped his perspective on ambition and success. Writing became his refuge, a way to explore how his experiences could inspire others.

Ideas began to take shape: a retreat center that blended nature and mindfulness, a platform combining technology with tools for self-reflection. These weren't just projects—they were extensions of the clarity he had found, ways to bridge the external and internal worlds.

As Amit boarded the bus back to the city, the villagers gathered to see him off. Their warmth and blessings stayed with him as the bus rumbled away, the golden fields of the village glowing in the afternoon light. He didn't know exactly what lay ahead, but for the first time, he wasn't afraid. Amit was no longer defined by the chase; he was defined by the journey—one rooted in intention, presence, and the quiet courage to embrace the unknown.

Because sometimes, stepping into the unknown is the only way to truly find ourselves.

THE DUALITY OF LAUGHTER AND TEARS

Conclusion of Part III: Beyond Dreams

As the chapters of Part III unfolded, Amit's journey illuminated a profound truth: life is not defined solely by the milestones we achieve, but by the meaning we create and the values we uphold along the way. This section marked a pivotal phase in his transformation, as he moved beyond the narrow confines of materialistic ambition to explore the depths of purpose, connection, and authenticity. It was a journey of rediscovery, one that challenged him to look inward and redefine what truly mattered.

The turning point—a personal crisis—acted as the fulcrum on which Amit's life began to pivot. This moment of reckoning was not merely a collision of relentless ambition with external realities but an awakening to the fragility of the life he had constructed. The foundation of his achievements, built on constant striving and external validation, suddenly felt precarious, unable to withstand the weight of what he truly yearned for: connection, balance, and a sense of inner peace.

In confronting this fragility, Amit found clarity. He began to see that goals and accomplishments, while valuable, are ultimately empty when untethered from the richness of human connection and the simple joys of living with intention. The crisis became his crucible, melting away illusions and hardening his resolve to build a life rooted in meaning rather than appearances.

Stepping away from his career and into the unknown was an act of courage, a leap of faith that required him to shed not just the security of his professional identity but also the expectations he had carried for so long. This journey was not just a physical departure from the familiar; it was a philosophical exploration of authenticity and purpose. Amit's time in the village, his encounters with monks, and the quiet moments of solitude in nature served as both a mirror and a guide, reflecting back the questions he had long avoided and pointing toward the answers he needed to find.

Through these experiences, Amit came to understand that fulfillment is not a destination reached through accomplishments or accolades. Instead, it is a state of being—one that is cultivated through mindful presence, intentional living, and the courage to embrace uncertainty. The external and internal, the material and spiritual, are not opposing forces but complementary aspects of a balanced life. Integration, he realized, is the key to true fulfillment.

Part III, *Beyond Dreams*, resonates as a universal challenge: the quest to transcend societal expectations and conventional definitions of success. Amit's story is a reminder that ambition, while a powerful motivator, must be tempered with purpose to avoid becoming an empty pursuit. In letting go—of rigid aspirations, of the need for control, and of the fear of failure—he discovered a new kind of freedom. This freedom was not about escaping responsibility but about realigning his life with values that nourished his soul.

Amit's journey in this part is a testament to the power of trust—trust in oneself, in the process of growth, and in the unknown. It is also an invitation to all of us to examine our own paths. Are the dreams we chase truly our own, or have they been shaped by societal pressures and expectations? Are we climbing ladders without questioning whether they are leaning

THE DUALITY OF LAUGHTER AND TEARS

against the right walls? Amit's story reminds us to ask these questions and to have the courage to seek answers that resonate deeply with who we are.

As Part III draws to a close, Amit stands not at the culmination of his transformation but at the threshold of a new chapter. He has traded the ceaseless pursuit of fleeting goals for a deeper exploration of life's intangible rewards: connection, presence, and authenticity. His dreams have not been abandoned but redefined, reshaped to align with the essence of his true self and the values he holds most dear.

The message of Part III is both simple and profound: to go beyond dreams is not to forsake them, but to expand their horizons. It is to redefine success not as a checklist of achievements but as a life lived in harmony with our deepest truths. In Amit's story, we find a call to reflect, to recalibrate, and to trust that the unknown holds the potential for extraordinary growth and fulfillment.

As this part concludes, we are left with a resonant truth: the most meaningful journeys are not about reaching a destination but about discovering who we become along the way. By embracing life's mysteries and living with intention, we can create a legacy not of trophies or titles but of authenticity, love, and purpose—one that transforms both ourselves and the world around us.

Part IV: The Fair of Life—Shared Joys and Sorrows

8: The Gathering

The sun dipped lower on the horizon, painting the sky with hues of amber and rose as Amit's bus rolled to a stop. The town ahead was alive, a canvas of swirling colors and vibrant energy that seemed to breathe with life. Banners stretched across narrow streets, their intricate patterns weaving stories of tradition and unity. The air carried the mingling scents of spices, incense, and the sweetness of sugar bubbling in oil. Rhythms of dhols and flutes reverberated through the town like a collective heartbeat, calling everyone toward the heart of the celebration.

Amit stepped off the bus, his senses immediately immersed in the life pulsating around him. The town square, just a short walk away, was a bustling hive of activity. Vendors shouted cheerfully from their stalls, offering trays of glistening jalebis, vibrant fabrics, and handcrafted trinkets. Children weaved through the crowd, their laughter cutting through the ambient chatter, while elders lingered on the fringes, their serene expressions reflecting the comfort of familiarity.

The villagers had spoken of this festival with reverence during Amit's stay in the hills, describing it as a time when barriers dissolved and the community came together to celebrate shared history and collective hope. Drawn by their words, Amit had decided to witness the event for himself, curious about what it might unveil—not just about the town, but about his own journey.

As Amit entered the square, he was struck by the atmosphere. Every corner was alive with a kaleidoscope of sights, sounds, and smells. Stalls lined the streets, their tables piled high with offerings—vividly dyed textiles, jars of tangy pickles, and jewelry that caught the light like shards of stars. A vendor expertly swirled batter into sizzling oil, producing golden jalebis that sent waves of sweetness through the air. Amit couldn't resist pausing to watch, mesmerized by the rhythm of his movements.

At the center of the square stood a stage adorned with vivid backdrops and strings of marigold. Performers in elaborate costumes danced with precision, their every step narrating tales that had been passed down through generations. The crowd erupted in applause and laughter, their joy a tangible presence that seemed to envelop Amit in its warmth.

Drawn by the aroma of cooking and the cheerful chatter of a group gathered nearby, Amit found himself at a communal cooking station. A massive pot of khichdi bubbled over an open fire, its golden hues shimmering as volunteers stirred it with large wooden ladles.

"Would you like to help?" a woman asked, handing him a knife and a handful of carrots.

Amit hesitated for only a moment. The simplicity of the invitation felt refreshing, untainted by expectation or pretense. "I'd love to," he replied, settling beside her.

As he peeled and chopped, Amit was struck by the camaraderie around him. Stories and laughter flowed freely, the group teasing one another with an ease that only familiarity

THE DUALITY OF LAUGHTER AND TEARS

could bring. A young boy described his adventures climbing trees, earning fond chuckles, while an elderly man recounted a story of a long-ago festival when a storm nearly swept the cooking pot away. Amit joined in the laughter, feeling a sense of belonging that was both unexpected and profoundly comforting.

When the food was ready, the volunteers served it to the crowd in simple leaf plates. Amit found a spot among strangers who quickly became friends, sharing the meal in a circle that radiated warmth. The khichdi, rich with spices and care, wasn't just nourishment; it was a testament to the collective spirit of the community.

As night descended, the festival took on a magical quality. Strings of fairy lights crisscrossed the square, their glow casting a soft, golden hue over the gathering. The stage became the focal point as musicians, dancers, and storytellers shared their talents with an eager audience.

Amit's attention was captured by an elderly singer whose haunting melody carried the weight of love, loss, and hope. Her voice seemed to pierce through the noise of life, reaching into the depths of every listener's soul. Tears welled in Amit's eyes as he felt her story resonate with his own journey—moments of doubt, longing, and the gradual rediscovery of purpose.

The storyteller who followed brought a sense of levity and reflection. His tale, about a village that overcame drought through unity and perseverance, mirrored the teachings Amit had encountered in the monastery. It was a reminder that challenges, no matter how daunting, were best faced together.

After the performances, Amit gravitated toward a small group gathered around a bonfire on the edge of the square.

They waved him over with unspoken warmth, handing him a cup of steaming chai as he settled into the circle.

The conversations were a blend of nostalgia and philosophy. A teacher spoke of the joy in seeing his students learn and grow, while a farmer reflected on the delicate balance between the land and the sky that sustained his livelihood. Their words were simple, yet they carried a depth that Amit found profoundly moving.

When it was his turn to share, Amit spoke of his own journey—of leaving behind a life defined by deadlines and accolades, of finding solace in simplicity, and of seeking a sense of purpose beyond achievement. The group listened intently, their nods and smiles encouraging him to continue.

A young woman, her eyes bright with conviction, added a thought that stayed with Amit long after. "Festivals like this remind us of our shared humanity," she said. "They teach us that life is not just about the struggles we endure or the goals we chase, but about the connections we make and the joy we find in each other's company."

Walking back to his guesthouse under a canopy of stars, Amit felt a profound sense of peace. The festival had been more than a celebration of culture; it had been a reminder of what truly mattered. In the shared meals, the stories exchanged by the fire, and the laughter that filled the air, Amit had glimpsed a truth he had long forgotten: that life's beauty lies not in isolation but in togetherness.

The gathering had illuminated the puzzle of life in a way that solitude never could. It showed Amit that meaning is not something to be found in individual pursuits but something

THE DUALITY OF LAUGHTER AND TEARS

pieced together through connection, community, and shared experiences.

As he lay in bed that night, the echoes of the festival still vivid in his mind, Amit felt a renewed sense of purpose. The road ahead remained uncertain, but he no longer feared the unknown. He had learned that the journey was not one he had to walk alone—and that, in finding each other, we find ourselves.

9: Stories Around the Fire

The fire crackled gently, its amber light flickering across the circle of faces gathered around it. Amit sat cross-legged on the ground, a steaming cup of chai warming his hands against the cool night air. Above, the stars stretched endlessly across the velvet sky, their brilliance offering a quiet contrast to the intimacy of the gathering below.

The group was a mosaic of lives and experiences: an elderly farmer with hands weathered by decades of labor, a young schoolteacher with a smile that invited trust, a cluster of teenagers stifling their giggles, and Amit, who had been drawn to the gathering by its unspoken promise of connection.

The fire seemed to hold a magnetic power, drawing out stories that might otherwise remain unspoken. It wasn't just a source of warmth but a space of vulnerability, where the soft glow illuminated not just faces but emotions, dreams, and shared humanity.

The farmer leaned forward, his hands resting on his knees as he began to speak. His voice, deep and gravelly, carried the cadence of someone accustomed to speaking sparingly but with purpose. His words unfolded a tale of hardship and resilience, painting a vivid picture of a drought that had tested the limits of his village.

THE DUALITY OF LAUGHTER AND TEARS

"It was the worst drought we'd ever seen," he began, his eyes fixed on the flames. "The fields turned to dust, and the wells ran dry. Livestock weakened, and hope withered alongside the crops."

His voice faltered for a moment, weighted by memory. "At first, we tried to endure it alone, each family guarding what little they had. But as the days stretched into weeks, and then months, we realized that survival wasn't something we could achieve on our own."

He described how the village came together, pooling resources and labor, digging deeper wells, and gathering each evening to pray. "The rain didn't just bring water," he said, his voice softening. "It brought life—life not only to our fields but to our spirits. That rain taught us something more profound: that no matter how hard life gets, we're stronger when we stand together."

As he finished, the group sat in contemplative silence, the fire crackling softly as if acknowledging the weight of his words. Amit found himself imagining the scene: the cracked earth drinking in the rain, the villagers embracing under the storm, their resilience borne from shared struggle.

The next story came from a woman in her thirties. Her voice was steady, though tinged with an undercurrent of pain that spoke of loss. "Six years ago," she began, "I lost my husband to an accident. It was sudden, cruel, and left me with two young boys to raise alone."

The group listened intently as she recounted the overwhelming grief and the seemingly insurmountable responsibilities that followed. "I didn't think I could make it," she admitted. "But the village didn't let me fall."

She described how her neighbors stepped in, bringing food, helping with her children, and tending to her farm. "It wasn't pity," she said with a bittersweet smile. "It was love—unquestioning, unwavering love. They reminded me that even in the darkest times, I wasn't alone."

Her words hung in the air, heavy with the truth of shared humanity. Amit felt a lump rise in his throat as he thought about his own moments of isolation, the times he had struggled silently, believing that vulnerability was a weakness. Her story was a reminder that strength is found not in solitude but in connection.

The tone lightened as a teenager, brimming with youthful enthusiasm, leaned forward to share his dream of becoming a teacher. His words were filled with the raw optimism of someone who hadn't yet faced the weight of life's realities. "I want to inspire others," he declared, glancing shyly at the schoolteacher sitting nearby.

The teacher smiled, his pride evident despite his humility. "Dreams are important," he said, his voice gentle yet firm. "But the journey to achieve them is what truly shapes us. And that journey is never walked alone."

The exchange drew smiles and quiet laughter from the group, but it also carried a profound truth. Amit reflected on his own journey, the mentors and connections that had shaped his path, and the moments of encouragement that had propelled him forward.

When it was Amit's turn to speak, he hesitated. The firelight reflected in his eyes as he finally began. "I suppose I should share why I'm here—not just at this festival, but on this journey."

THE DUALITY OF LAUGHTER AND TEARS

He spoke of his former life, of the success and recognition that had once defined him but had ultimately left him hollow. "I thought I was living the dream," he admitted, "but I was so consumed by achievement that I lost sight of what really mattered. It wasn't until my father's health scare that I stopped to ask myself the questions I'd been avoiding: Who am I beyond my work? What do I truly value?"

The group listened in silence, their faces illuminated by the fire's warm glow. Encouraged, Amit continued, his voice growing steadier. "What I've learned is that life's meaning isn't found in the answers but in the connections we make and the questions we dare to ask. It's in moments like this—gathered around a fire, sharing our stories—that we find what truly matters."

The schoolteacher nodded thoughtfully, his voice breaking the silence. "Joy and sorrow," he said, "are two halves of a whole. They're meant to be shared. That's what makes life rich—not avoiding pain or chasing happiness, but embracing both together."

As the night wore on, the group's conversations ebbed and flowed, the fire's embers glowing like fading stars. Amit felt a quiet gratitude for the openness and wisdom shared around the fire. Each story had been unique, yet they all carried a common thread: the understanding that life's burdens and blessings are best borne together.

Amit realized that he had spent much of his life chasing individual success, believing that fulfillment came from standing alone at the peak of achievement. But here, among strangers whose stories had woven into his own, he saw the truth: life's meaning is found not in solitude but in connection.

As the group dispersed, bidding each other goodnight, Amit lingered by the dying fire. The warmth of the flames had faded, but their glow remained—a quiet reminder of the bonds forged in their light.

For Amit, the evening had been more than a series of stories. It had been a lesson in shared humanity, a reminder that life's greatest joys and deepest sorrows are not meant to be faced alone. They are the threads that bind us together, creating a tapestry of experiences that give life its richness and meaning.

As he rose to leave, the night air cool against his skin, Amit felt a quiet resolve settle within him. His journey was far from over, but he was beginning to understand that its purpose wasn't in finding answers. It was in sharing the journey—with its joys, sorrows, and uncertainties—with others. And in doing so, discovering what it truly meant to live.

10: A Mirror to the Soul

By the next morning, the festival had fully bloomed into a kaleidoscope of color and energy. The main square thrummed with life, every corner teeming with activity. Vendors enthusiastically hawked their goods, their voices adding to the lively symphony of chatter, music, and laughter. Performers in elaborate costumes weaved through the streets, drawing curious onlookers with their graceful movements and bursts of theatrical flair. Families and friends strolled through the crowd, their faces radiant with excitement as they immersed themselves in the festivities.

The stalls that lined the square brimmed with an astonishing variety of treasures. Handcrafted jewelry sparkled like tiny constellations against velvet displays, each piece reflecting the dedication of its maker. Clay pottery in earthy tones showcased the elegance of simplicity, while bolts of embroidered fabric hung like vibrant banners, shimmering as they caught the sunlight. The air was a sensory feast, rich with the mingling aromas of sizzling pakoras, fresh jalebis, marigold garlands, and the faint smokiness of incense drifting from the temple nearby.

Children darted through the crowd, their laughter rising like music. They clutched colorful balloons, their faces alight with unrestrained joy that seemed to infuse the air with an infectious lightness. Amit smiled as he absorbed the scene, his heart swelling with a sense of renewal that had eluded him for years.

For much of the festival, Amit had been content to observe, moving through the vibrant tapestry of stalls and performances as a quiet spectator. But on this day, something stirred within him—a desire to step out of his detached role and immerse himself fully in the rhythm of the celebration.

He noticed a group of volunteers struggling to set up a game booth in one corner of the square. A woman balanced a clipboard in one hand while trying to fasten garlands with the other, her movements a mix of determination and exasperation. Nearby, a man wrestled with a banner that flapped stubbornly in the breeze.

Without hesitation, Amit approached. "Need some help?" he asked, his voice cutting through the chaos.

The woman looked up, relief flashing across her face. "Absolutely," she said, handing him the garlands with a grateful smile. "We're short on hands for the charity stalls. The work isn't glamorous, but it matters."

Amit rolled up his sleeves and dove in, finding himself quickly swept into the current of activity. Together, they secured the flapping banner, arranged prizes for the games, and reorganized the cluttered booth. With each small task, Amit felt a growing sense of purpose.

Every action seemed to hold significance. Hanging the banner wasn't just about decoration—it was an invitation for joy. Guiding a lost child to their parents wasn't a chore—it was a chance to bring comfort. Restocking shelves wasn't

THE DUALITY OF LAUGHTER AND TEARS

mundane—it ensured someone would find exactly what they needed.

As the day progressed, Amit found himself stationed at a ring toss booth. The simple game quickly became a hotspot of laughter and friendly competition. Children cheered as they aimed for the pegs, parents clapped in encouragement, and friends teased each other with playful jabs.

It was here that Amit experienced a moment that would linger with him long after the festival ended. A young boy, no older than six, approached the booth clutching a single coin in his small hand. His wide eyes scanned the array of prizes, finally settling on a plush elephant nearly as large as he was.

"That one," the boy whispered shyly, pointing at the elephant.

"Great choice," Amit said, crouching to meet the boy's gaze. "Let's see if we can win it."

The boy's first toss missed, as did the next two. His confidence wavered, and his small shoulders slumped in disappointment. But Amit, sensing the boy's dismay, leaned closer and offered an encouraging smile. "You're getting better with each try," he said gently. "One more. You've got this."

The boy took a deep breath and tossed the ring. It landed squarely on the peg. His face lit up with uncontainable joy, and he squealed with delight as Amit handed him the elephant. The boy clutched the plush toy tightly, his grin a beam of pure happiness as he ran off to show his parents.

Watching him go, Amit felt an unexpected surge of emotion. It wasn't just the boy's excitement that moved him—it was the knowledge that his small effort had made a difference. The fulfillment he felt in that moment was profound and unfamiliar, unconnected to accolades or achievements. It came from connection, from giving, from being present.

The festival wasn't just a celebration; it was a microcosm of life. Each interaction, no matter how fleeting, wove a thread into the fabric of the day. Amit handed out plates of steaming food at a bustling stall, carried supplies for an elderly vendor, and even joined a group of performers for an impromptu dance that left the crowd cheering.

These acts, seemingly insignificant on their own, accumulated into something far greater. Amit marveled at how different this felt from his old life. In the corporate world, every action had been tied to outcomes, every effort measured by its return. Here, contribution was untethered from expectation. It was about giving freely, about being part of a community, about sharing joy for its own sake.

As evening descended, the square transformed into a luminous wonderland. Lanterns of every shape and color illuminated the scene, casting a warm, golden glow. The chatter of the crowd mingled with the gentle hum of evening performances, creating a harmony that resonated deeply within Amit.

He found a quiet spot on the temple steps, his body tired but his spirit light. Watching the lanterns sway in the soft breeze, Amit reflected on the day. He thought about the boy clutching his elephant, the elderly vendor's gratitude, the collective laughter during the dance. Each moment had been a reminder of a truth he was only beginning to grasp: fulfillment wasn't about taking—it was about giving.

THE DUALITY OF LAUGHTER AND TEARS

The festival, with its vibrant chaos and quiet beauty, had held up a mirror to Amit's soul. For so long, he had equated success with personal achievement. But here, amidst the laughter and connection of the festival, he had rediscovered the joy of communal involvement.

Philosophy: The Fulfillment of Giving

Amit's realization marked a profound turning point: the understanding that life's deepest and most enduring rewards are not found in the heights we climb alone, but in the moments when we reach out to others. The festival, with its radiant energy and interconnected spirit, had been a revelation—a living reminder that fulfillment is not measured by individual achievements but by the connections we nurture and the joy we create together.

As Amit reflected on the stories shared around the bonfire, the laughter of children, and the collective effort of the cooking circle, he saw a universal truth unfold before him. Fulfillment, he realized, is a product of giving—of offering our time, our attention, and our kindness to others without expectation. It is in these moments of giving that we bridge the gaps between us, creating ripples of impact that extend far beyond what we can see or imagine.

Empathy, Amit now understood, is the thread that binds us as a human family. The act of giving—whether through service, a listening ear, or even a quiet gesture of encouragement—holds the power to transform not just others, but ourselves. It dissolves barriers, softens the edges of our individual struggles, and reminds us that we are all part of a greater whole.

As the lanterns flickered against the darkening sky, their soft glow casting warm shadows across the square, Amit felt an unexpected sense of peace settle over him. The questions that had driven him to leave his old life—questions about purpose, fulfillment, and the meaning of success—no longer weighed heavily on him. In their place was a simple but profound truth:

THE DUALITY OF LAUGHTER AND TEARS

the act of giving had anchored him, grounding him in a sense of purpose that transcended the pursuit of answers.

Amit's thoughts returned to the festival, to the small but significant moments that had unfolded throughout the day. The shared laughter over a communal meal, the stories of resilience and hope exchanged between strangers, the collective joy of dancing under the stars—these were not grand gestures or monumental achievements, but they carried a richness and depth that no accolade could match. They were the moments that illuminated life's true meaning.

As he walked through the square one last time, the vibrant energy of the festival beginning to fade into the quiet of the night, Amit felt a renewed sense of purpose take root within him. He realized that the greatest journeys in life are not those of conquest or ambition, but of connection—journeys where we learn to see ourselves as part of something larger, where we build not for ourselves but alongside others.

Life's meaning, Amit thought, is not found in the monuments we construct to our own success, but in the bridges we build to one another. It is in the shared moments of joy and sorrow, the acts of kindness that ripple outward, and the spaces where empathy transforms relationships into community. In giving, we discover not just the beauty of the world but the fullness of our own humanity.

In that realization, Amit found not an ending but the beginning of a new chapter. It was a chapter defined not by ambition but by presence, not by the relentless pursuit of milestones but by the richness of moments shared. It was a chapter that shifted the focus from taking to giving, from striving to connecting, and from individual triumphs to collective harmony.

As he stepped out into the quiet of the night, the echoes of the festival still resonating in his heart, Amit carried with him a sense of peace he hadn't felt in years. The path ahead was still uncertain, but he now understood that it wasn't the destination that mattered—it was the journey of connection, compassion, and shared purpose that made the journey worthwhile.

The flickering lanterns faded into the distance, but their light remained within him, a beacon guiding him forward. And as Amit walked on, he felt ready to embrace a life where the act of giving, the beauty of connection, and the joy of presence were the true measures of success.

THE DUALITY OF LAUGHTER AND TEARS

Conclusion: Part IV – The Fair of Life: Shared Joys and Sorrows

Part IV encapsulates the essence of life as a shared journey, where the threads of connection weave a tapestry richer and more meaningful than anything forged in solitude. Through the vivid and transformative experience of the festival, Amit encounters a world that challenges the isolation and relentless ambition of his former existence. The vibrant town, with its bustling streets, communal celebrations, and moments of raw human connection, becomes a powerful metaphor for the truth he had long been seeking: life is meant to be lived together.

Themes Revisited

Life as a Collective Experience In *The Gathering*, Amit steps into the heart of a cultural festival, discovering the vibrancy of communal living. The festival's kaleidoscope of sights, sounds, and emotions serves as a microcosm of life itself. Every interaction—whether with strangers or in the roles he takes as a volunteer—underscores the interconnectedness of human stories. Through these connections, Amit realizes that life gains depth and meaning when shared, and that our individual narratives are enriched by the collective.

Sharing Joy and Sorrow In *Stories Around the Fire*, Amit listens to heartfelt tales from the locals—stories of resilience in the face of drought, love amidst loss, and triumph despite adversity. These narratives reveal a universal truth: joy and sorrow are intertwined, and it is in their sharing that we find strength, healing, and understanding. Whether through tears or laughter, these moments of connection remind Amit that life is not defined by events but by the relationships and communities that help us navigate them.

The Fulfillment of Communal Involvement In *A Mirror to the Soul*, Amit dives into the festival as a volunteer, discovering the profound joy of giving and being present for others. The seemingly simple acts—helping a child win a prize, assisting a vendor, or sharing a smile—become deeply meaningful. Through these experiences, Amit uncovers the transformative power of empathy and communal involvement. The joy of contributing to others' happiness nourishes not only those he helps but also his own sense of purpose, grounding him in a renewed connection to humanity.

Amit's Transformation

This chapter of Amit's journey marks a profound shift in his understanding of life's purpose. The festival is no longer just an event; it becomes a mirror, reflecting back his capacity for empathy, joy, and connection. For the first time, he sees that life's deepest meaning is not found in solitary pursuits or material accomplishments but in the shared experiences that bind us together.

Through the stories he hears, the relationships he builds, and the acts of service he performs, Amit begins to embrace the idea that fulfillment lies in the collective journey. He learns to be fully present, to appreciate life's highs and lows as part of a shared human experience, and to find joy in the moments that connect us to one another.

Looking Forward

As Amit leaves the festival, he carries its lessons with him—a renewed commitment to building a life rooted in connection, empathy, and shared joy. He understands now that fulfillment is not a solitary achievement but a communal celebration. It is found in the imperfect, beautiful chaos of human connection, in the joy of giving, and in the strength that comes from standing together.

The fair has given Amit a roadmap for his journey ahead. It has shown him the value of togetherness, the power of giving as much as receiving, and the richness of a life intertwined with others. It is a reminder that in the puzzle of life, the pieces come together not through solitary effort but through the bonds we form, the stories we share, and the collective joys and sorrows that give life its color and meaning.

Part IV: A Final Reflection

Part IV leaves Amit—and the reader—with a profound realization: life is not a solitary pursuit of milestones but a shared experience of connection. The festival becomes a metaphor for the fair of life itself, a place where joys and sorrows are mingled and amplified through community. It reminds us that our greatest strengths, our deepest joys, and our most enduring meanings are found in the collective journey we share.

As Amit steps into the next chapter of his life, he carries with him the wisdom of the fair: that the purpose of life is not in perfect answers but in the imperfect beauty of shared humanity. It is this realization that transforms him, offering a sense of direction for a life lived with open hands, open hearts, and a renewed embrace of the world around him.

Part V: Choosing Silence and the Path of Solitude

11: The Silent Retreat

The mountain air was crisp and invigorating as Amit arrived at the retreat center, hidden within the tranquil folds of a remote valley. The journey to this secluded haven had been long, the winding path offering glimpses of snow-capped peaks and emerald forests, but nothing could have prepared him for the profound silence that greeted him. This silence was not empty—it was alive, a stillness that resonated with the mysteries of the surrounding mountains and seemed to invite introspection.

The retreat center was simple yet serene, its wooden cabins arranged in a circle around a central meditation hall. Nearby, a small stream wove its way through the grounds, its gentle gurgling the only sound breaking the silence. As Amit stepped through the gates, he felt a mix of anticipation and unease. He had come here seeking clarity, but he knew the silence would demand he confront truths he had long avoided.

Entering Silence

The retreat began in the modest meditation hall, its unadorned walls bathed in soft morning light. The participants sat on cushions arranged in a semicircle, facing the head instructor—a monk in saffron robes whose presence radiated calm authority. His gaze moved across the group, not in judgment but in a quiet acknowledgment of their shared purpose.

"Welcome," the monk began, his voice deliberate and soothing. "Each of you has come here seeking something—peace, clarity, perhaps even escape. Whatever brought you here, let silence be your guide."

He outlined the structure of the retreat: ten days of complete silence. There would be no speaking, no writing or reading, no digital distractions, and no interaction with others—not even through gestures or eye contact. The daily routine was simple yet rigorous, consisting of meditation, light physical tasks, and silent meals.

"Silence," the monk explained, "is not the absence of sound but the presence of awareness. It allows us to hear the thoughts we suppress, to feel the emotions we avoid, and to uncover the truths hidden within us. In silence, we meet ourselves."

Amit felt a knot tighten in his chest. The prospect of ten days without his usual distractions was both liberating and intimidating. The monk seemed to sense the group's apprehension.

"Some of you may find silence uncomfortable, even overwhelming," he said. "But remember, silence is not your adversary. It is a mirror. It reflects your thoughts, your fears, your desires. Observe them. Let them come and go like clouds passing through the sky. In this way, you will begin to understand yourself."

The Early Struggles

The first few days of silence tested Amit in ways he hadn't anticipated. The absence of external noise amplified the chatter within his mind. Memories, anxieties, and unfinished thoughts rose unbidden, like an unstoppable tide. Without the usual distractions of work, conversation, or screens, he was left alone with the chaos of his thoughts.

During meditation sessions, he found himself reliving moments of regret and insecurity—times when he had failed to meet his own expectations or sought validation through achievements. The relentless self-criticism was exhausting. His restlessness spilled into the structured activities, making even simple tasks feel burdensome.

The silence, which he had romanticized as serene, felt oppressive. The urge to escape, to pick up a phone or talk to someone, was almost unbearable. Yet the retreat's rules held him firmly in place, forcing him to confront the discomfort head-on.

Shifting Perspectives

On the third day, something shifted. Amit stopped resisting his thoughts and began observing them as the monk had instructed. He let his memories and emotions arise without judgment, picturing them as waves crashing against the shore—powerful, but transient.

One vivid memory emerged: a professional triumph that had left him feeling inexplicably hollow. He recalled smiling at the praise he received, yet inwardly grappling with a sense of emptiness. As he allowed the memory to linger, he realized that his suffering wasn't rooted in the event itself but in his relentless need for external validation.

This insight was transformative. Amit began to see his thoughts as stories he told himself—narratives shaped by fear, guilt, and unexamined desires. By observing these thoughts without becoming entangled in them, he felt a growing sense of detachment. The storm of his mind began to calm, and moments of stillness emerged, fleeting but profound.

Finding Peace in Presence

By the fifth day, the silence no longer felt like an adversary but an ally. Amit started to notice the details of his surroundings with newfound clarity—the texture of the wooden floor, the rhythm of his breath, the interplay of light and shadow in the meditation hall. Each moment became an opportunity to be fully present.

Afternoon walks around the retreat grounds became his favorite practice. He marveled at the intricate patterns of moss on tree trunks, the gentle sway of grass in the wind, and the stream's effortless flow over smooth stones. The natural world seemed to mirror his inner journey, teaching him the value of flowing with life rather than resisting it.

Insights and Transformation

The retreat became a mirror, reflecting the fears and desires that had driven Amit's relentless pursuit of success. He saw how much of his ambition had been fueled by a need to prove his worth—to himself and others. But in the stillness of the retreat, he began to release these burdens.

Amit realized that true fulfillment wasn't about achieving milestones or meeting external expectations. It was about aligning his actions with his values and finding joy in the present moment. The silence revealed a deeper purpose—not to conquer life but to live it with authenticity and grace.

Emerging from Silence

On the tenth day, the silence was lifted. As participants shared their reflections, Amit hesitated. Speaking felt strange

THE DUALITY OF LAUGHTER AND TEARS

after days of quiet, as if breaking the silence would disrupt the clarity he had found. When he finally spoke, his voice was steady but reflective.

"Silence," he said, "is like a bridge to yourself. It's not always easy to cross, but what you find on the other side is worth it. It reveals not only what you hide from the world but also what you hide from yourself."

The monk, listening intently, nodded with a serene smile. "Silence doesn't change you," he replied. "It reveals you."

The Journey Ahead

As Amit descended the mountain, the world felt sharper, more vibrant. The lessons of the retreat were etched into his soul: the importance of stillness, the power of presence, and the strength that comes from embracing vulnerability.

He no longer felt the need to chase an elusive ideal of success. Instead, he was grounded in the knowledge that his worth was not tied to external achievements but to the integrity of his actions and the depth of his connections.

The retreat had been more than a pause—it was a turning point, a reminder that silence is not an escape but a space for profound discovery. As Amit stepped back into the world, he carried with him a quiet resolve: to live with awareness, to embrace both the light and the shadows within, and to trust in the unfolding journey of life.

Philosophy: Embracing Silence to Find Clarity

Silence, Amit came to understand, is not simply the absence of noise; it is an active presence, a space that holds within it the possibility of profound transformation. It is a sanctuary where the noise of the world—and the relentless chatter of the mind—fades into the background, allowing the deeper truths of the soul to emerge. For Amit, embracing silence meant more than just stepping away from the external chaos; it meant confronting the internal storms he had long avoided.

In the stillness of his retreats and solitary moments, Amit faced the fears, desires, and unresolved emotions that had silently guided his actions for years. He realized that much of his life had been shaped by patterns he had never paused to examine—a drive for achievement that masked a fear of inadequacy, and a relentless pace that kept him from addressing the questions he feared to ask.

The silence was not easy. It stripped away the distractions he had used to shield himself, exposing him to the rawness of his own humanity. But it was in this exposure that the seeds of clarity were planted. By confronting what he had buried, Amit found the courage to let go of the old patterns that no longer served him and to embrace a life more aligned with his truest self.

In silence, Amit learned the art of listening—not just to the world around him but to the subtle, often-overlooked whispers within. He began to hear the wisdom in his own thoughts and emotions, the lessons hidden in his struggles, and the quiet but persistent voice of intuition that had been drowned out by the noise of daily life. This practice of deep

THE DUALITY OF LAUGHTER AND TEARS

listening became his compass, guiding him not just in moments of stillness but in the inevitable chaos of everyday existence.

The clarity Amit found was not the result of sudden revelations or neatly packaged answers. It came from the willingness to ask the right questions and the patience to sit with what arose in response. Silence became the space where those questions could breathe, where possibilities could unfold without the pressure of immediate resolution.

Amit's journey offers a powerful reminder: clarity is not something we find by seeking harder or running faster. It is something we create by slowing down, by allowing ourselves the time and space to reflect. In a world that prizes productivity and constant motion, silence is a radical act of self-care—a way to reconnect with the essence of who we are and what truly matters.

Through his experience, Amit discovered that silence is not an escape from life but an entry point into its deepest truths. It is a teacher, a mirror, and a guide. It showed him that clarity is not about having all the answers but about being present enough to hear the questions. And it revealed that authenticity is not something we achieve by reaching outward but something we uncover by turning inward.

As Amit carried this lesson forward, he found that silence had reshaped his approach to life. In meetings and conversations, he listened more and spoke less, creating space for others to share their truths. In moments of conflict, he paused before reacting, allowing the wisdom of stillness to inform his response. And in the quieter corners of his days, he continued to nurture his relationship with silence, trusting it to guide him toward clarity and purpose.

The philosophy of embracing silence is not about retreating from the world but about engaging with it more fully. It teaches us that within the quiet, there is a vast richness—a wealth of insight, understanding, and peace that we can access if we are willing to slow down and listen. It reminds us that the answers we seek are often already within us, waiting to be heard.

Amit's journey is a testament to the transformative power of silence. It shows us that in letting go of noise—both external and internal—we open ourselves to the clarity, courage, and authenticity that lead to a life of deeper meaning. Silence, far from being a void, is the foundation of all understanding. It is the space where we can finally meet ourselves.

12: The Solitary Path

The road stretched endlessly before Amit as he left the village behind, its winding curves carving through the quiet landscape. The vibrant energy of the festival and the retreat still lingered in his mind, like the fading notes of a beautiful song, but with each step, a growing sense of isolation crept in. The warmth of shared meals, the camaraderie of strangers, and the quiet revelations of the retreat gave way to an expansive silence that now felt foreboding.

Amit was alone, and for the first time since starting his journey, solitude felt like a weight rather than a gift.

The Burden of Loneliness

In the days that followed, Amit's journey began to feel like a test of endurance. The picturesque towns he passed through blurred together, their quiet streets and modest guesthouses offering little solace. Without the structured discipline of the retreat or the communal vibrancy of the festival, he was left to confront the raw intensity of his own thoughts.

Nights in unfamiliar rooms became especially challenging. One evening, he sat in a small, dimly lit space—a place as nondescript as his own growing sense of detachment. A single candle flickered on the table, its flame casting restless shadows on the walls. The silence that had once been soothing now seemed oppressive, amplifying every doubt and fear lurking within.

Memories of his life at Lumina emerged with startling clarity. He could almost hear the hum of office chatter, the rhythmic tapping of keyboards, and the celebratory applause that followed a successful pitch. He saw himself surrounded by his team, their faces lit with the shared excitement of solving a complex problem. The pull of these memories was strong, and for a fleeting moment, Amit longed to return to that life.

The familiar offered comfort: the respect of his peers, the satisfaction of tangible achievements, and the predictable rhythm of a 9-to-5 existence. He imagined calling his colleagues, explaining his change of heart, and seamlessly stepping back into the life he had left behind. The thought brought a temporary sense of relief, like a warm blanket against the chill of uncertainty.

But then, just as quickly, the deeper reasons for his departure surfaced. Amit remembered the emptiness that had persisted despite his success—the gnawing sense that something essential was missing. He had walked away from Lumina not out of dissatisfaction with his work but because he yearned for a clarity and purpose that his professional life could not provide.

Returning to that life might have eased his discomfort temporarily, but Amit knew it wouldn't bring the fulfillment he sought. The security of the familiar was seductive, but it was a false promise—a distraction from the deeper work he needed to do.

The Test of Commitment

THE DUALITY OF LAUGHTER AND TEARS

Amit spent hours grappling with his thoughts, the flickering candle his only companion. He wrestled with the tension between the pull of security and the call to growth. On one side was the promise of stability and recognition; on the other was the uncertain path of self-discovery, fraught with challenges but ripe with potential.

In those moments of doubt, Amit reflected on the lessons he had learned at the retreat and the stories of resilience he had heard at the festival. He thought about the stream that had taught him the importance of flow, the silent nights that had revealed his fears, and the quiet strength he had begun to cultivate within himself.

Growth, he realized, wasn't found in avoiding discomfort but in moving through it. The familiar might have offered refuge, but it would also have confined him to the patterns he was trying to break. With a deep breath, Amit extinguished the candle, plunging the room into darkness. The path ahead was unclear, but he resolved to continue.

A Journey of Reflection

The loneliness Amit felt wasn't merely the absence of companionship—it was an encounter with his deepest self. In the stillness of solitary nights, his thoughts became louder and more insistent. Memories of joy, regret, vulnerability, and resilience surfaced with startling clarity, demanding his attention.

He revisited moments of triumph and loss, of love and missed opportunities. These memories weren't just fragments of his past; they were signposts, each pointing to unexamined parts of himself. The solitude stripped away the distractions of daily life, leaving him exposed to questions he had long avoided: Who was he beyond his achievements? What did he truly value?

At first, the introspection felt like a burden. The weight of self-examination was heavy, and Amit often found himself yearning for the comforting noise of his previous life. But gradually, he began to see the solitude as something more—a teacher. It wasn't there to punish him but to guide him, to strip away the layers of external validation and reveal the core of who he was.

The Power of Small Moments

As Amit moved through new towns and landscapes, he began to notice the world around him with fresh eyes. The smallest details took on profound meaning—a sunrise spreading golden light over a valley, the intricate patterns of leaves fluttering in the wind, the quiet melody of a stranger's laughter.

These moments, once overlooked, became his anchors. They reminded him that life's beauty wasn't confined to grand achievements or monumental events. It existed in the quiet, unassuming experiences of everyday life.

Amit also found solace in fleeting human connections: a shopkeeper's kindness, a child's spontaneous laughter, the harmony of voices singing around a village bonfire. These encounters, though brief, nourished his spirit and reminded him that while his path was solitary, he wasn't truly alone.

Choosing the Unknown

One day, Amit passed through a bustling marketplace. The noise and energy felt overwhelming after days of quiet reflection, but a café with a television caught his eye. On the screen, a former colleague spoke passionately about a project Amit had helped conceive at Lumina.

For a moment, the allure of his old life resurfaced. He imagined himself back in the office, surrounded by his team, his name attached to success. The temptation was strong, but as he stood there, another memory emerged: the emptiness he had felt despite the accolades, the nights spent wondering if this was all there was.

Amit turned away from the café, each step a reaffirmation of his choice. The pull of the familiar was real, but his commitment to the path of self-discovery was stronger. He realized that the longing for his old life wasn't a call to return—it was a reminder of how far he had come.

The Strength in Solitude

Amit began to see his journey not as an ordeal but as an unfolding process. The doubts and temptations he faced weren't obstacles; they were opportunities to deepen his understanding of himself. Each challenge tested his resolve, but it also strengthened his commitment to authenticity.

The path of self-discovery wasn't about arriving at a destination. It was about embracing the journey, with all its uncertainties and lessons. Amit learned to find peace not in the absence of struggle but in the willingness to face it.

Philosophy: The Transformative Power of Solitude

The solitary path Amit walked was a profound challenge but also a transformative opportunity. It demanded courage to face the discomfort of self-examination and the humility to accept that growth was an ongoing process.

Through solitude, Amit discovered the value of silence—not as a void, but as a space for truth to emerge. He learned that self-discovery wasn't about achieving perfection but about embracing authenticity. It was about listening deeply, not just to his own thoughts but to the world around him.

By choosing solitude, Amit chose himself—not the version of himself shaped by external expectations, but the one that existed in the quiet spaces, free to evolve and grow. His journey was a testament to the strength found in vulnerability, the wisdom gained through introspection, and the beauty of embracing life's uncertainties.

As he continued down the winding road, Amit carried these lessons with him. The path ahead was still unknown, but for the first time, that felt like enough.

13: Embracing the Puzzle

The sun rose slowly over the horizon as Amit stood at the edge of a cliff, gazing at a valley cloaked in morning mist. The landscape stretched endlessly before him, a mosaic of rolling hills, meandering rivers, and scattered villages. The cool air carried the faint scent of dew and earth, and as the first rays of light painted the world in shades of gold, Amit closed his eyes and took a deep breath. For the first time in years, he felt no urgency—no compulsion to plan the future, solve unanswered questions, or chase elusive milestones.

In that moment, Amit wasn't striving for understanding; he was simply present, immersed in the quiet beauty of the world around him.

Shifting Perspectives

For much of his life, Amit had been driven by questions that loomed large and insistent: *Who am I? What is my purpose? How do I find fulfillment?* These questions had shaped every step of his journey, from leaving the security of his career to seeking clarity in festivals, retreats, and solitude. They had been both his guiding force and his heaviest burden.

But as the sunlight touched the valley below, something shifted within him. Amit realized that the answers he sought might never come in the neat, definitive form he had expected. The more he had tried to force clarity, the more elusive it had become. And now, standing on the edge of the unknown, he began to see that perhaps the beauty of life lay not in its answers but in its questions.

Life, he reflected, wasn't a problem to be solved but a puzzle—complex, dynamic, and endlessly intriguing. Like any puzzle, some pieces fell into place effortlessly, while others defied understanding, their purpose and connection remaining a mystery. The puzzle's value, Amit realized, wasn't in completing it but in engaging with it. It was the act of curiosity, exploration, and discovery that gave it meaning.

This realization was liberating. For so long, Amit had approached life as a challenge to conquer, its questions obstacles to overcome. Now, he saw them as invitations—to think, to grow, to connect. Each unanswered question became an open door, a possibility waiting to unfold.

The Puzzle's Pieces

Amit's thoughts drifted to the moments and stories that had shaped his journey. The resilience of the farmer during a drought, the widow's strength in rebuilding her life, the boy's unbridled hope—all these experiences had left indelible marks on him. They were pieces of the puzzle, each unique and meaningful in its own right.

He thought of the retreat, where silence had stripped away the noise of his mind and revealed truths he hadn't dared to confront. He recalled the connections he had formed along the way—the strangers who had shared their kindness, the fleeting conversations that had sparked unexpected insights. These, too, were pieces of the puzzle, woven into the tapestry of his journey.

THE DUALITY OF LAUGHTER AND TEARS

As Amit pieced together these fragments, he felt a profound sense of acceptance. The puzzle would never be complete, and that was okay. Its beauty lay in its incompleteness, in the ever-present opportunity to discover, to connect, and to create.

Letting Go of Certainty

For much of his life, Amit had equated happiness with certainty—with knowing who he was, what he wanted, and where he was going. Ambiguity had been something to avoid, a source of discomfort that stood in the way of peace. But now, standing on the edge of the valley, he saw ambiguity in a new light.

The questions that had once burdened him—*Who am I? What is my purpose?*—were no longer obstacles to overcome. Instead, they became companions on his journey, guiding him toward deeper exploration and growth. The unpredictability of life, once a source of frustration, now felt like its greatest gift.

Amit thought of the creative processes he had always admired: a musician improvising a melody, a painter adding brushstrokes to an unfinished canvas, a child playing without concern for rules or outcomes. None of these acts required completeness to be meaningful. Their beauty lay in their spontaneity, in the joy of creation and discovery.

Perhaps, Amit thought, life was much the same. It didn't need to follow a rigid path or reach a definitive destination to be fulfilling. Its value lay in the unfolding, in the process of engaging with each moment as it came.

The Joy of the Incomplete

This shift in perspective brought Amit a sense of liberation he had never before experienced. The relentless need to have all the answers, to map out a perfect life, had been an invisible weight pressing down on him for years. But now, he felt an unfamiliar lightness, as if that burden had dissolved into the ether. Life no longer needed to fit into a neat narrative or rigid plan. Instead, he embraced its unfolding, trusting that the path ahead would reveal itself, step by step, as he journeyed forward.

For Amit, this newfound freedom came with a revelation: the beauty of life lay not in its perfection but in its imperfection. The gaps, uncertainties, and moments of incompleteness were not flaws to be corrected but spaces to be cherished. They were the silences between notes that made the music richer, the blank spaces on the canvas that gave depth to the painting.

He began to notice the quiet joys of life in ways he never had before. On a misty morning, the intricate patterns of a spider's web caught his eye, its dewdrops glinting like tiny jewels in the sunlight. Amit paused, marveling at the fragility and artistry of something so fleeting. Later, the gentle warmth of sunlight on his skin during a cold day filled him with an inexplicable sense of gratitude. The sight of children playing tag in a dusty village square—unrestrained, their laughter spilling into the air—stirred in him a sense of wonder he hadn't felt since his own childhood.

These small, incomplete moments carried a profound power. They weren't milestones or achievements, but they enriched his life in ways he couldn't quantify. Each moment felt like a piece of a puzzle, valuable not for how it completed the picture but for the depth and color it brought to the whole.

Amit realized that he had spent much of his life chasing the grand, overarching narratives—the perfect career, the ideal

THE DUALITY OF LAUGHTER AND TEARS

future, the flawless sense of purpose. In doing so, he had often overlooked the smaller threads that wove the fabric of meaning. Now, he saw that life's truest richness came from these threads—the fleeting moments of connection, the brief encounters of wonder, and the gentle presence of simply being alive.

The joy of the incomplete became a philosophy that shaped Amit's journey. He stopped striving for mastery over every situation and began allowing life to unfold naturally. This wasn't a surrender to complacency but an embrace of curiosity and openness. He saw the unknown not as something to fear but as a landscape filled with possibility. The ambiguity he had once fought against became an invitation to explore, to engage, and to grow.

In this new way of living, Amit discovered that incompleteness wasn't a sign of failure but a marker of life's endless potential. A spider's web could never be permanent—it would tear and rebuild, reflecting the cycle of creation and impermanence. The laughter of children wasn't an achievement; it was an expression of pure, unbridled joy. And the warmth of sunlight wasn't a goal to attain but a gift to be savored in the moment.

As Amit continued his journey, he found that this philosophy extended beyond his personal experiences. It shaped how he viewed relationships, work, and the world itself. Relationships didn't need to be perfect to be meaningful; their complexity was part of their beauty. Work didn't have to provide all the answers; its value lay in the effort, growth, and connections it fostered. And the world didn't need to be fully understood; its mystery was part of what made it worth exploring.

The joy of the incomplete taught Amit that life wasn't about finding closure in every chapter or certainty in every decision. It was about engaging with the process, appreciating the unfolding, and finding wonder in the unfinished. Each moment, no matter how small or fleeting, carried within it the potential to expand his understanding of the world and his place within it.

As Amit reflected on his journey, he saw that embracing incompleteness had transformed his relationship with himself and the world. The pressure to be perfect, to know everything, to control the future, had been replaced by a profound sense of peace. He didn't need to have it all figured out. It was enough to be present, to live with intention, and to trust in the beauty of life's imperfections.

The joy of the incomplete wasn't just a lesson for Amit—it was an invitation for all of us. To pause in the rush of life. To notice the intricate patterns of a spider's web. To feel the warmth of sunlight. To hear the laughter of children and let it remind us of the wonder we once knew. It was a call to embrace life not as a puzzle to be solved but as an ever-changing mosaic to be experienced, one imperfect, beautiful piece at a time.

THE DUALITY OF LAUGHTER AND TEARS

Philosophy: The Puzzle of Life

As Amit continued his journey, he came to embrace the puzzle of life not as something to solve but as something to experience. The unanswered questions, the rough edges, the incomplete pieces—they weren't flaws. They were what made the puzzle dynamic, alive, and endlessly fascinating.

Choosing to live without all the answers wasn't an act of resignation; it was an act of courage. It required him to let go of the illusion of control and to trust in the natural unfolding of life. It was a testament to the beauty of imperfection, to the richness that came from engaging with life's complexities and contradictions.

The puzzle of life was ever-changing, its pieces shifting with time. Amit understood now that its value lay not in its completion but in the act of living it—of embracing the questions, cherishing the connections, and finding joy in the journey.

As the sun climbed higher in the sky, bathing the valley in light, Amit felt a deep sense of gratitude. He didn't need to see the full picture or have all the answers. It was enough to live the questions, to explore the unknown, and to trust in the unfolding of his journey.

Standing on the edge of the valley, Amit embraced the puzzle of life with an open heart. And as he took his first step forward into the day, he carried with him the quiet joy of knowing that the beauty of life wasn't in its resolution but in its infinite possibilities.

SANDEEP CHAVAN

Conclusion of Part V: Choosing Silence and the Path of Solitude

The journey into silence and solitude was a crucible for Amit, stripping away the noise of the world and, more profoundly, the noise within himself. The retreat in the mountains had dismantled his distractions, leaving him alone with thoughts and emotions long buried. In the stillness, Amit encountered a mirror that reflected his fears, desires, and deeply ingrained patterns. Yet, it was within this vulnerable space that he discovered the transformative power of truly listening—not just to the external world, but to his own authentic voice.

The solitary path that followed was no less challenging. Without the structured rhythm of the retreat or the support of a community, Amit faced moments of profound loneliness and inner conflict. The allure of his old life called to him, tempting him with its familiar comfort and certainty. But through these trials, he cultivated resilience. What once seemed an adversary—loneliness—revealed itself as a patient teacher. Amit learned that true peace is not found in the validation of others or the warmth of companionship but in the quiet acceptance of one's own company.

By the time Amit reached the point of embracing life's inherent ambiguity, he had undergone a profound transformation. The questions that had once loomed over him as burdens—*Who am I? What is my purpose?*—were no longer weights to bear but companions to explore. They guided him not toward resolution but toward curiosity and wonder. Amit realized that the beauty of life lay not in its answers but in its mysteries—the gaps, the rough edges, the unfinished pieces of the puzzle. Life, he came to understand, wasn't something to be solved but something to be lived.

Embracing the Essence of the Journey

This chapter of Amit's journey revealed a pivotal truth: the path of self-discovery is as much about letting go as it is about finding. It requires releasing the need for certainty, embracing the unknown, and surrendering to the process itself. Silence and solitude, though daunting at first, offered Amit clarity and strength. They helped him see that life is not a linear path to a destination but an ever-unfolding journey, rich with challenges, beauty, and limitless possibilities.

In solitude, Amit found not isolation but empowerment. The silence that once felt oppressive became expansive, a space in which he could listen deeply, both to the world around him and to the truths within. The absence of external distractions illuminated the richness of the present moment, teaching him that fulfillment isn't tied to outcomes or achievements but arises from engaging with life as it is.

Moving Forward

As Amit continued on his path, he carried a newfound sense of peace—not because he had resolved all his questions, but because he had learned to live them. The solitude that once felt heavy was now a source of strength, and the silence he had resisted became a sanctuary. Amit was no longer running—from his past or toward an imagined future. Instead, he was walking with intention, fully present, embracing the beauty and complexity of life's puzzle one step at a time.

Choosing silence and solitude wasn't an escape; it was a choice to face life's uncertainties with courage and openness. It was a decision to trust in the unfolding journey, to accept the ambiguity of existence, and to find meaning not in arriving but in experiencing. And in that choice, Amit found the freedom to truly live.

THE DUALITY OF LAUGHTER AND TEARS

Epilogue: The Ongoing Journey

14: The Return Home

The midday sun hung brightly in the sky as Amit stepped off the train, his bag slung over his shoulder. The familiar hum of the city greeted him—a cacophony of honking cars, street vendors calling out their wares, and the rhythmic murmur of countless conversations. Once, he had drifted through this symphony without much thought, consumed by deadlines and ambitions. Now, it was overwhelming in its intensity yet strikingly beautiful in its harmony.

The streets he had once navigated with haste now felt vibrant with purpose. The laughter of children playing in the park reached his ears, blending with the hiss of steam from a chai vendor pouring tea into clay cups. Faces moved past him, each etched with their own stories, and sunlight filtered through the sprawling branches of a peepal tree. Everything felt alive, interconnected, like a tapestry of moments he was finally beginning to understand.

Reconnecting with Family

When Amit reached his parents' house, the scent of home-cooked food greeted him before the door even opened—a familiar blend of spices and comfort that carried with it a lifetime of memories.

THE DUALITY OF LAUGHTER AND TEARS

His mother pulled him into a tight embrace, her hands lingering as if to convince herself he was really there. "You've lost weight," she said with mock reproach, though her teary eyes gave away her relief.

"I'm fine, Ma," Amit reassured her, his voice warm. "But I have missed your cooking."

His father, quieter but equally moved, placed a hand on Amit's shoulder—a gesture that spoke of unspoken pride and affection.

Anika, his younger sister, appeared in the hallway and immediately teased him about his new beard. "You went away a stressed-out businessman and came back looking like a sage. When do we get to see you in saffron robes?"

Amit laughed, the sound unfamiliar yet comforting in his own ears. "Not quite there yet," he replied, letting her drag him inside.

Over dinner, the house came alive with animated chatter. Amit listened more than he spoke, savoring the familiar rhythm of his family's voices. His mother filled him in on neighborhood gossip, his father shared cricket updates, and Anika recounted her children's antics.

When the conversation turned to him, Amit hesitated. He shared glimpses of his journey—not in dramatic revelations but as quiet reflections. He spoke of the vibrant festival where strangers had become companions, the mountain retreat where silence had become his teacher, and the solitary paths where loneliness had transformed into clarity.

"Did you find what you were looking for?" his father asked, his tone gentle yet probing.

Amit paused, letting the question settle before answering. "I didn't find answers," he said, his voice steady. "But I've learned to live the questions."

His father nodded thoughtfully, his expression softening. "That's all anyone can really hope for," he replied.

Rediscovering Joy in the Everyday

In the days that followed, Amit found joy in the simple moments he had once overlooked. He kneaded dough in the kitchen under his mother's watchful eye, laughing at her playful critiques. He played cricket in the alley with Anika's children, their giggles echoing through the narrow streets. Evenings were spent on the terrace with his father, sipping chai and discussing everything from family history to the mysteries of life.

Each moment, ordinary on the surface, held an extraordinary depth. They were the threads of a life he had once been too busy to notice, now woven into a tapestry of meaning and connection.

Amit also began to reintegrate himself into the world he had left behind. At Lumina, he stepped into the role of advisor and mentor, focusing on fostering balance and purpose within the company. He introduced mindfulness sessions for the team, encouraging them to pause and reflect amidst the chaos of their schedules.

"Success," he told them one day, "isn't just about what we achieve but how we achieve it. It's about the people we become along the way."

THE DUALITY OF LAUGHTER AND TEARS

He spearheaded initiatives that emphasized connection and empathy, such as a mentorship program pairing seasoned employees with new hires. The focus was not merely professional growth but mutual understanding and support.

Beyond work, Amit devoted time to volunteering. He taught at a community center and helped organize local events, finding fulfillment in giving back. These moments of service, small but meaningful, reminded him of the festival where he had first felt the profound joy of shared purpose.

A Quiet Evening on the Terrace

One evening, Amit sat alone on the terrace, gazing out at the city. The lights shimmered like stars, creating a mosaic of lives and stories. A soft breeze brushed his face as he looked up at the sky, the constellations scattered like pieces of a celestial puzzle.

He thought of the laughter and tears that had marked his journey, the connections he had made, and the solitude he had embraced. Each moment, whether joyous or painful, had shaped him. Amit realized that life wasn't about avoiding sorrow or chasing joy but about embracing both as integral parts of the human experience.

The puzzle of life, he reflected, was never meant to be complete. Its beauty lay in its imperfections, in the way its pieces came together in surprising and sometimes inexplicable ways. Each fragment—a moment of connection, a lesson learned, or an act of kindness—added richness to the whole.

Sipping his chai, Amit felt a profound sense of peace. He didn't have all the answers, but he didn't need them. Life's value wasn't in its resolution but in the experience of living it—piece by piece, moment by moment.

Philosophy: A New Way of Being

Amit's return home marked not an ending but the beginning of a new chapter. The wisdom he had sought on distant paths was never as far away as he had believed. It was woven into the everyday moments, the simple acts of kindness, and the connections he had cultivated.

He carried with him profound lessons:

- **Silence reveals truth.** In quiet spaces, Amit found the strength to confront his fears and desires, uncovering his authentic self.
- **Loneliness teaches resilience.** The solitude he once feared became a space for growth and self-reliance.
- **Questions hold value.** Amit no longer sought to solve life's puzzles but to live them, finding meaning in the exploration.
- **Joy and sorrow are intertwined.** Life's beauty lay in its contrasts, each emotion enriching the other.

These lessons became the foundation of Amit's new way of being. He had let go of the need to control every outcome, embracing life's complexity and trusting in its unfolding.

THE DUALITY OF LAUGHTER AND TEARS

The Road Ahead

As the city hummed softly below, Amit whispered to himself, "This is enough." It wasn't resignation but peace—peace in knowing that life didn't need to be perfect or fully understood to be deeply appreciated.

The puzzle of life was far from complete, and that incompleteness was its greatest gift. Each day held the promise of new questions, new connections, and new moments to cherish.

Amit closed his eyes, carrying with him the hum of the city—a rhythm of laughter and tears, silence and connection, puzzles and possibilities. He didn't need to see the whole picture to trust its beauty.

All he needed was the courage to keep living it, one piece at a time.

A Message to My Readers

Dear Reader,

Life, as I have come to understand it, is a puzzle—beautiful, intricate, and often bewildering. It doesn't come with a clear guide or a set of instructions. It's a journey filled with moments of laughter that warm your soul and tears that carve wisdom into your heart. The pieces don't always fit neatly, and some may never find their place. But that's the essence of it—that's what makes life so profoundly meaningful.

We live in a world where the mind is often restless, chasing dreams and striving for goals. It's easy to get caught up in the pursuit, believing that fulfillment lies just beyond the next milestone. But what if the chase itself is not the point? What if, instead of running toward a distant horizon, we pause to appreciate the path beneath our feet?

Through the pages of this book, I've shared Amit's journey—his triumphs and struggles, his moments of solitude and connection. His story mirrors the experiences we all share: the pull of ambition, the weight of expectations, and the yearning for something deeper. It's a reminder that life isn't about solving its puzzle but engaging with it. The beauty lies in the imperfections, the unanswered questions, and the courage to live without needing to know it all.

THE DUALITY OF LAUGHTER AND TEARS

Our lives, like the fairs we attend, are gatherings of moments, people, and experiences. We are not meant to walk this journey alone. The laughter of friends, the stories shared around a fire, and the silent support of loved ones during hard times—these are the threads that weave the fabric of our lives. They teach us that even in our solitude, we are connected.

Silence, too, has its lessons. It allows us to confront ourselves, to hear the whispers of our soul that are often drowned out by the noise of the world. Choosing silence is not about withdrawal but about presence—being fully aware of who we are and what truly matters. It is in these quiet spaces that we find the strength to embrace life's puzzle, piece by piece.

And so, dear reader, I leave you with this thought: life's greatest wisdom lies not in its answers but in its questions. It is in the journey, not the destination, that we discover our purpose. Laughter and tears, joy and sorrow—they are not opposites but companions, each enriching the other and adding depth to the story of our lives.

Thank you for walking with me through this book, for reflecting on these ideas, and for engaging with the puzzle of life alongside me. I hope it has offered you a moment of pause, a spark of insight, or a whisper of encouragement to embrace your own journey with an open heart.

With gratitude,

Sandeep Chavan

Don't miss out!

Visit the website below and you can sign up to receive emails whenever SANDEEP CHAVAN publishes a new book. There's no charge and no obligation.

https://books2read.com/r/B-A-EPGPC-AQPJF

BOOKS2READ

Connecting independent readers to independent writers.

Did you love *The Duality of Laughter and Tears*? Then you should read *It's Not AI, It's AHI - Amplified Human Intelligence*[1] by SANDEEP CHAVAN!

It's Not Just AI, It's AHI: The Amplified Human Intelligence by **Er. Sandeep Chavan** offers a deep dive into the future of artificial intelligence, focusing on how AI can amplify human intelligence (AHI) to enhance our lives and potential. This book moves beyond the sensationalism of AI as a threat or autonomous entity, instead framing AI as a tool for amplifying human capabilities across industries and everyday life.

---

1. https://books2read.com/u/3Rjvrn

2. https://books2read.com/u/3Rjvrn

Chavan, an experienced engineer with over two decades of experience in AI and education, demystifies AI by presenting its real-world applications and showing how AHI enhances cognitive, emotional, and decision-making skills. The book walks readers through the transformational impact of AI in key sectors like healthcare, finance, education, engineering, and manufacturing. In these sectors, AI is not replacing human intelligence but working alongside it—improving diagnostic accuracy, optimizing financial decisions, providing personalized learning, and enhancing precision and productivity in manufacturing.

The heart of this book emphasizes that human creativity, ethics, and emotional intelligence are irreplaceable. AI, while a powerful amplifier, relies on human input for nuanced thinking, creativity, and ethical judgment. The book explains how human involvement is crucial in ensuring AI systems are fair, ethical, and aligned with our values.

Chapters on the ethical dimensions of AI highlight the responsibility of developers and the powerful role of tech leaders in shaping AI's future. Chavan calls out the dangers of hype and the myths around AI superintelligence, explaining why human intelligence remains central to AI's evolution and how AI's amplification of human potential is the true focus.

In the final chapters, Chavan looks ahead, predicting how AHI will evolve over the next decades, urging societies to steer AI development toward collective benefit. The book envisions a future where AI and human intelligence fully integrate, creating a world where both work in harmony to solve complex challenges and drive innovation.

With a focus on technical depth, ethics, and the future of AHI, this book is a must-read for tech professionals, educators, students, and anyone interested in the future of AI. Chavan's thoughtful and practical approach guides readers through understanding AI as a tool to amplify human potential, making this a key resource for shaping the future of human-AI collaboration.

Read more at https://www.sandeepjchavan.com/.

Also by SANDEEP CHAVAN

Ultra Modern Life Philosophy
The Duality of Laughter and Tears

Standalone
It's Not AI, It's AHI - Amplified Human Intelligence
The Decision Paradox
The Four Sapiens
Malicious Script of Indian Polity
The IIT Legacy & Global Impact
The IIT Legacy & Global Impact
You are just a Version of Your Original
Win the Game You Didn't Choose
Always Keep Your Bags Packed
Reveal to Shield - Learn the Game of Facades
Engage Beyond Elections
Culture, Identity & Change: The Evolution of Indian Society
The Triangular Dynamics
Never Trust Without Doubt
If You Can't Change the Country, Leave the Country

Live Fearless with Fear
India: The Investment Magnet

Watch for more at https://www.sandeepjchavan.com/.

About the Author

Sandeep Chavan is a globally recognized author and an acclaimed industrial engineer with an impressive career spanning over two decades. He has worked with leading multinational companies, contributing significantly to their operations in industrial engineering, manufacturing, and technology. In addition to his extensive professional background, Chavan is a celebrated thought leader in a diverse range of subjects, including world economics, emerging technologies, investment strategies, and educational reformation.

His bestselling works explore complex subjects like the Indian economy, the philosophy of personal growth, and the dynamics of decision-making, providing clear insights to readers from all walks of life. Sandeep has also been a passionate educator, conducting numerous seminars and workshops for students and professionals, helping them navigate the modern world's challenges. Known for his ability to break down intricate topics, he has written extensively on subjects like finance, investments, and motivation, influencing countless individuals across the globe.

Sandeep Chavan's books serve as a guide for personal and professional transformation, blending his expertise in engineering with his profound understanding of philosophy and human potential. His unique perspective and experience make him a standout figure in today's literary and industrial landscape.

Read more at https://www.sandeepjchavan.com/.

www.ingramcontent.com/pod-product-compliance
Ingram Content Group UK Ltd.
Pitfield, Milton Keynes, MK11 3LW, UK
UKHW031954131224
452403UK00010B/582